PREDESTINATION

and the

SAINTS' PERSEVERANCE,

STATED AND DEFENDED

from the objections of Arminians, in a review
of two sermons, published by
Rev. Russell Reneau.

****

BY REV. P. H. MELL,

**Professor of Greek and Latin,
Mercer University, Ga.**

Reprinted by the Wicket Gate. The Wicket Gate is a journal of biblical and historical theology and is produced quarterly by Grace Baptist Fellowship.

The Wicket Gate is funded from two sources: a nominal subscription fee and the voluntary gifts of those interested in the work.

Editors: Robert Paul Martin
           C. Ben Mitchell

Editorial Advisory Board: Thomas K. Ascol,
     Carolyn Wilson Green, Marvin Jones,
     Fred A. Malone, Robert L. Mounts,
     Tom J. Nettles, Ernest C. Reisinger,
     David A. Sapp

Editorial Secretary: Nancy B. Mitchell

Subscription Secretary: Deborah S. Martin

P. H. Mell -- Defender of the Faith Once Delivered to the Saints

In an age when both polemics and strong doctrine are greeted with less than grateful praise, and those who engage in either are viewed with suspicion, the republication of the present work may appear to be somewhat of an anomaly. However, an age whose main symptom is repulsion to such traits needs the strong medicine of both. Furthermore, when such an antidote pours from the pen of one as highly esteemed in his own age as Patrick Hues Mell, a double potency should accompany its internalization.

Mell, born in Liberty County, Georgia, July 19, 1814, held more official positions in Baptist life at every level than any other Southern Baptist in history. The following table demonstrates the universal approval enjoyed by Mell among his contemporaries. [P. H. Mell, Jr., Life of Patrick Hues Mell. (Louisville: Baptist Book Concern, 1895), p. 151.]

ABILITIES AS A PRESIDING OFFICER
TABLE OF RECORD

Years	Ga. Association	Ga. Baptist Con.	Sou. Baptist Con.
1845-46	Clerk	Clerk	
1847	Clerk	Clerk	
1848	Clerk	Clerk	
1849	Clerk	Clerk	
1850	Clerk	Clerk	
1851	Clerk	Clerk	
1852		Clerk	Dr. Mell was one of the original delegates present at Augusta when the Southern Baptist Convention was first organized. (1845)
1853		Clerk	
1854		Clerk	
1855	Moderator	Clerk	
1856	Moderator		
1857	Moderator	President	
1858	Moderator	President	
1859	Moderator	President	
1860	Moderator	President	
1861	Moderator	President	
1862	Moderator	President	
1863	In the army	President	President.
1864	Moderator	President	No Convention.
1865	Moderator	No Convention	No Convention.

3

1866....	Moderator	President	President.
1867....	Moderator	President	President.
1868....	Moderator	President	President.
1869....	Moderator	President	President.
1870....	Moderator	President	President.
1871....	Absent by sickness	President	President.
1872....	Absent by sickness	Absent by sickness	Absent by sickness.
1873....	Absent by sickness	Absent by sickness	Absent by sickness
1874....	Moderator	Absent by sickness	Absent by sickness
1875....	Moderator	Absent by sickness	Absent by sickness
1876....	Moderator	Absent by sickness	Absent by sickness
1877....	Moderator	President	Absent by sickness
1878....	Moderator	President	Absent by sickness
1879....	Moderator	President	Absent by sickness
1880....	Moderator	President	President.
1881....	Moderator	President	President.
1882....	Moderator	President	President.
1883....	Moderator	President	President.
1884....	Moderator	President	President.
1885....	Moderator	President	President.
1886....	Moderator	President	President.

Known as the "Prince of Parliamentarians", Mell's acceptance among his peers did not arise solely from his great gifts as a moderator. In addition, his firm theological conviction, viewed as Baptist orthodoxy, and his inimitable ability in lucid expression of theological themes combined to endear him to Baptists as an able conductor of Baptist meetings.

Not only did Mell's parliamentary abilities and theological expertise qualify him among Baptists, his long acquaintance with country churches in Georgia kept his sensitivities close to the concerns of the ordinary church people. His pastorates included tenures of ten years at Greensborough Church in Penfield, Georgia, twenty-eight years in Oglethorpe at Antioch Church, and thirty-three years at Bairdstown Church between Green and Oglethorp counties.

His preaching ministry found more than adequate academic complement as he served in positions of higher education from 1842 until his death in 1888. For approximately thirteen years he was Professor of Ancient Languages at Mercer University. That connection was dissolved somewhat painfully in 1855, but, in 1856, he was elected Professor of Ancient Languages at the State University of Georgia located in Athens. In 1860 he assumed two new positions: one, he taught metaphysics and ethics, and, two, he became vice-chancellor. In 1878 he ascended to the position of chancellor, which he maintained until his death.

Other honorable positions in Baptist life were offered to Mell. He was twice elected president of Mississippi College, once elected secretary of the Southern Baptist Publication Society, once elected president of Wake Forest, once elected president of Georgetown, once elected president of Cherokee College at Carsville, Georgia, once elected president of Montgomery Female Institute, and was called to the pastorate of First Baptist Church in Savannah, Georgia. All of these positions he refused.

As a preacher, Mell focused on the doctrines he loved dearly. His method of preaching was designed to give greatest weight to the dignity and wonder of the subject matter. His son, P. H. Mell, Jr., described his father's manner.

> The little thirty-minute sermons that some preachers offer to an already over-fed congregation pale beside the matchless discourses he used to give the crowds at Antioch and Bairdstown. His slender, lithe figure rose in its strength; his piercing eyes glowed or melted in tender pathos as his mind grasped the glorious truths of the Gospel; he held his hearers spellbound many times a full hour, and, if the theme was unusually grand, and far-reaching in its fuller development, he stood for an hour and a half, and yet his people never thought he preached long. He started out by stating his propositions clearly and distinctly, and then proceeded to bring forward and support them with such an array of argument and of Scriptural authority, and clothed his ideas in language so plain, so simple, so strong, so beautiful, that the truth was fixed in the minds of his listeners. (Ibid, pp. 64-65)

Cathcart's Baptist Encyclopedia adds the following evaluation of Mell's preaching.

> The power and penetration of his intellect enable him to grasp a doctrine forcibly and present it clearly; and his skill in the art of thinking and reasoning is so great that he always speaks logically, his conclusions having the force of demonstrations.

Preaching as Mell practiced it was a tool for correcting error and inculcating truth. Mrs. D. B. Fitzgerald, a member of the Antioch Church and a resident in Mell's home for a number of years, recalls Mell's initial efforts at the church.

> When first called to take charge of the church Dr. Mell found it in a sad state of confusion. He said a number of members were drifting off into Arminianism. He loved the truth too well to blow hot and cold with the same breath. It was a Baptist church and it must have doctrines peculiar to that denomination preached to it. And with that boldness, clearness, and vigor of speech that marked him, he preached to them the doctrines of predestination, election, free-grace, etc. He said it was always his business to preach the truth as he found it in God's Word, and leave the matter there, feeling that God would take care of the results. (Ibid., pp. 58-59.)

As indicated in Mell's preface to the present work, he lamented the tendency of some Baptist preachers to ignore clear expositions of the Doctrines of Grace in their public ministrations. Others, to Mell's sorrow, "have even preached... doctrines not consistent with (the Doctrines of Grace), others have given them only a cold and half-hearted assent, and some few have openly derided and denounced them." This melancholy situation arose from misinformation on the one hand and ignorance on the other. Therefore, Mell sought to remedy the ignorance and "to counteract, as far as I was able, the tendencies to Arminianism" he observed around him.

In short, though this particular treatise was prompted by the challenge to Calvinism so boldly promulgated by one Russell Reneau, Mell's real motivation issued from his conviction that Arminianism was really not just a different emphasis, but a different gospel. The difference between traditional Arminianism and traditional Calvinism consists not in the supposition that the former emphasized man's part and the latter God's part; in fact, both have much to say about the relative parts played by the sinful creature and the holy creator. A positive difference in substance forms the real impasse between the two. Arminianism assumes an equality of God's grace toward any number of sinners, some of which will be saved and some of which will remain lost. Wherein lies the difference? Man's choice becomes the deciding factor between heaven and hell. Therefore, in answer to Paul's question, "Who makes thee to differ from another?" the Arminian, consistent with his system, must answer "I do."

The Calvinist, however, states that salvation is truly of the Lord. Only a particular distinguishing grace makes one sinner to differ from another. Grace consists not merely of a provision and offer of eternal life but actually operates to make alive the dead sinner and bring him to repentance and faith. The faith by which righteousness comes is granted no less than the righteousness itself. Mell's succinct statement of these truths demonstrates a lucidity of thought and cogency of argument few could parallel in his day, or since. Seeing election and reprobation as only two particular manifestations of the comprehensive sovereignty of God, he expressed their essence and relationship in the following way.

In reference to men, predestination is divided into two parts: 1st, as it relates to the elect, and 2nd, as it relates to the non-elect. Having decreed to create a world, and to people it with beings who would voluntarily sin against him, he determined from eternity to save some, and to leave others to perish in their sins. "Willing to show his wrath, and to make his power known," he "endured with much longsuffering" these as "the vessels of wrath fitted to destruction: and that he might make known the riches of his glory on" those as "the vessels of mercy which he had afore prepared unto glory."
Rom 9:22,23.

To carry out his purpose of grace, he chose some to holiness and eternal life, entered, for their sake, into the Covenant of Redemption with the Son and the Holy Ghost, appointed his Son as their substitute, to suffer in their stead, and, having died to rise again, and appear as their advocate before his throne, appointed all the intermediate means necessary, and, by an infallible decree, made their salvation sure. Those, "whose names are not written in the book of life" (Rev. 20:15), who are "appointed to wrath" (I Thes. 5:9), who were "before of old ordained to condemnation" (Jude 4) who would "stumble at the word, being disobedient, whereunto also they were appointed" (I Peter 2:8), he determined to leave in their sins, and to endure them with much longsuffering as vessels of wrath fitted to destruction.

While, by an immutable decree, He has made all things in time fixed and sure, all this occurs in perfect consistency with the free agency of the creature, and God is not the author of sin. --The elect are, by the influence of sovereign grace, made willing in the day of God's power and those not elected have no active principle of disobedience imparted to them, and feel no restraint upon their wills--they are simply passed by, and permitted to follow the inclinations of their own hearts.(Rev. P.H. Mell, Predestination and the Saints' Perseverance Stated and Defended. Charleston: Southern Baptist Publication Society, 1851, pp. 26-27.)

His love for and exposition of these truths were not forsaken in later life. The last sermon he ever preached, December 12, 1887, dealt with Divine election. His text was II Thessalonians 2:13,14:

But we are bound to give thanks alway to God for you, brethren beloved of the Lord, because God hath from the beginning chosen you to salvation through sanctification of the Spirit and belief of the truth: Whereunto he called you by our gospel, to the obtaining of the glory of our Lord Jesus Christ.

Mell died in his home January 26, 1888, after several weeks of increasing weakness. Three days before his death he said, "I have been a wonderful child of providence, if not a child of Grace." At intermittent times during the last days he said: "For me to live is Christ, to die is gain. God is good and gracious and merciful -- merciful to sinners." "I commit my soul to God in Christ Jesus -- Glory be to God." "Once I was dead, but now am alive. In the other world I am thoroughly understood and thoroughly appreciated."

At the Southern Baptist Convention session in 1888, the Foreign Mission Board presented a memorial tribute to Mell. The introductory paragraph captured their estimation of his traits and influence.

The late President of the Southern Baptist Convention will be long remembered. His erect figure, angular features, keen eye, concise speech, his incisive thoughts, cogent logic, unyielding orthodoxy, commanding address, all represented a type of manhood which impresses indelibly even as steel makes cuts into granite not to be worn away by the waves of time. (Life of Patrick Hues Mell, p. 255.)

With a prayer that that estimation of Mell's abiding influence may again have reason to be uttered, the present volume is issued. The hopes for it extend no further than the author's hopes at its original publication.

> Should this publication have the effect to confirm my brethren in the faith once delivered to the Saints, and serve, in any degree, to counteract the tendencies, in our midst to Arminianism, I shall have accomplished my main design in writing.

SYNOPSIS AND OUTLINE

The following outline and synopsis of this pamphlet may aid the reader in grasping its organization. The whole consists of four facts: First, a discussion of the absurdity of Reneau's intent as well as method; second, a clear statement of the doctrine of predestination in its comprehensive meaning; third, a discussion of Reneau's first sermon on predestination; fourth, a discussion of Reneau's attempt to discredit the doctrine of perseverance of the saints.

I. This first section demonstrates Mell's elevated and intellectual sense of humor and engages in benevolent sarcasm toward Mr. Reneau in an effort to free him from self-delusion and unjustified arrogance. Throughout this section Mell seeks to expose three severe problems of his antagonist.

    A. His unbounded arrogance

    B. His lack of perception and/or candor in representation of arguments

    C. His tacitley blasphemous view of the authority of divine revelation

II. Mell gives a clear statement of the doctrine of predestination.

    A. Definition of predestination

        1. Seven propositions related to God's sovereignty as creator

        2. Three propositions related to God's role as upholder

        3. Three propositions related to God's sovereignty as governor

    B. How predestination relates to men

        1. The elect

        2. The non-elect (reprobate)

    C. Two remarks about the doctrine of predestination

        1. Remark 1 - objection as easily applied to Arminianism

        2. Remark 2 - difficulty arises out of two

considerations

    a. Thoughts of God too human

    b. False understanding of what "dishonors" God

D. Demonstrations or proofs of predestination

   1. Position 1 - God has intimate acquaintance with all His works

    a. Upholds

    b. Provides

    c. Disposes and governs

   2. Position 2 - in these relations God governs himself by a determinate plan

   3. Position 3 - this determinate plan existed from all eternity

   4. Conclusion - "predestination comes in like a flood" and includes all the events and means leading to the salvation of the elect and condemnation of the reprobate

  E. Objections to predestination

   1. God author of sin - Arminians have same problem

    a. Biblical examples

     1) Fall

     2) Joseph

     3) Crucifixion

     4) Other scriptures

    b. Arguments from reason

     1) Distinction between sinful act and the result attained

     2) If result is good it is worthy of him

      a) Two more objections

      b) Two more answers

2. Sinner exonerated

3. Destroys free agency

4. Makes God respector of persons

5. God unjust and cruel

   a. Preterition - God passes by some

   b. Condemnation - God punishes them

6. Makes use of means unnecessary

F. Practical benefits

   1. Tends to produce humility

   2. Tends to produce more earnest labor

   3. Tends to strengthen in the calamities of life

   4. Tends to excite gratitude to God

III. Consideration of the arguments of Reneau's first sermon.

A. Discussion of foreknowledge

   1. Simple intelligence

   2. <u>Scientia visionis</u>

      a. Differences between Calvinists and Arminians on foreknowledge

      b. Representation of Reneau's misunderstanding of foreknowledge

B. Discussion of Reneau's misunderstanding of unconditional election.

   1. Relation of election to moral character

   2. Comparison between Arminian and Calvinist views of election

   3. Relation of election to effectual calling as viewed by Arminians and Calvinists respectively

   4. Refutation of Reneau's objections to Calvinistic view of election (2)

   5. Mell demonstrates positive weaknesses of

Reneau's view

    a.   Equality of work of Spirit with all men

    b.   Elected because of foreseen faith

    c.   Elected subsequent to faith

    d.   Is faith a good work?

    e.   Is election always effectual or might it, in the end, be unavailing?

IV. The Doctrine of Perseverance

    A.   Two questions for discussion

        1.   Can Christians totally fall from grace?

        2.   Can Christians finally fall from grace?

    B. Discussion of Question A

        1.   Example of David

            a.   Clarifies the issue by five questions

            b.   Two considerations

                1) David did not apostatize as evidenced by repentance and faith

                2) Renewed man does not lose grace evidenced by I John 3:9 and the example of Peter

            c.   Discussion of the particulars of David's case

                1) The nature of grace

                2) The nature of the Cross

        2.   Universalism and perfectionism

    C.   Discussion of Question B

        1.   List of eight categories from which Calvinists argue for perseverance

        2.   Only two of these assailed by Reneau

            a.   Covenant of grace

            b.   Atonement

3. Scriptural arguments against perseverance by Reneau

    a. 2 Corinthians 6:1

    b. Parabolic material

       1) Matthew 5:13

       2) Matthew 12:43

       3) John 15:1-11

    c. I Corinthians 10:1-12

    d. 2 Peter 2:20-22

    e. I Chronicles 28:9

    f. Ezekiel 18:24

4. Examples of apostacy given in Scripture according to Reneau

    a. Adam and David recovered

    b. Judas

       1) Given to Christ   John 17:12

       2) Regenerated   Matthew 19:28

       3) Familiar friend   Psalm 41:9

    c. Hymeneus and Alexander

Tom J. Nettles
Memphis, Tennessee

PREFACE

The following tract appeared, first, in weekly numbers, in the columns of "The Christian Index", and is republished, with slight alteration and addition, at the request of many brethren. The controversial feature is retained, not because it is thought that Mr. Reneau's name will add any dignity to it, but because,

1. I have not time to re-write it.

2. If all allusion to Mr. R's publication were removed, it would lack congruity and completeness. It discusses Predestination and the Saint's Perseverance, because they are the doctrines assailed; and it is ostensibly confined to a consideration of Mr. Reneau's arguments.

3. Those who have requested its re-publication desire it to retain its original form. Mr. R's production, which it reviews, has been extensively distributed through parts of Georgia and Tennessee and has been lauded as a complete refutation of Calvinism. It is thought, therefore, that, in such localities, it is better calculated to do good in its present form. Besides, men are more likely to read an argument when it is associated with controversy than when it is presented in the form of abstract discussion.

I have been pained to notice, for some years past, on the part of some of our ministers, in some localities in the South, a disposition to waive the doctrines of Grace in their public ministrations. While some have been entirely silent about them and have even preached, though not ostensibly, doctrines not consistent with them, others have given them only a cold and half-hearted assent, and some few have openly derided and denounced them. This, in many cases, has resulted, doubtless, from a lack of information and from an apprehension, therefore, that the doctrines of Grace are synonymous with Antinomianism. For this reason, I have thought that a concise and popular exposition of those doctrines was urgently demanded. It is true, there are many able treatises on them, extant; but, they are all locked up in voluminous Bodies of Divinity and, therefore, not accessible to the general reader. I confess, then, that it was to supply, to the extent of my ability, this demand and to counteract, as far as I was able, the tendencies to Arminianism, that I took up my pen. For this purpose, I was glad that the pretext of answering Mr. Reneau was afforded me; and, with this object in view, I extended the discussion on the subject of Predestination beyond Mr. R's objections. Should this publication have the effect to confirm my brethren in the faith once delivered to the Saints and serve, in any degree, to counteract the tendencies in our midst to Arminianism, I shall have accomplished my main design in writing.

Of course, it will be understood that the term, Calvinism, is used in conformity to custom and not to imply that the doctrines embraced in it originated with the Genevan Reformer.

MERCER UNIVERSITY, GA., DECEMBER, 1850

PREDESTINATION AND
SAINTS' PERSEVERANCE

SECTION I

THE SUBSTANCE OF TWO DISCOURSES ON PREDESTINATION AND ON RECEIVING THE GRACE OF GOD IN VAIN, preached at several Camp grounds in the State of Georgia,in 1849, by Russell Reneau. Oxford, Ga. - Office of the Southern Family Journal. 1849

Religious controversy should never, without pressing necessity, be entered into. However pure may be the motives, which, at first, influence the combatants on both sides, and however unexceptionable the manner in which the discussion may be conducted, it is next to impossible to confine it to the naked question at issue, and it seldom, if ever, fails to be unprofitable to those engaged in it. Stimulated by knowing that they are contending under the eye of their respective friends, whose cause is entrusted to their hands, and too proud to consent to appear inferior to their opponents, they are too often tempted to lose sight of the glory of God and to struggle merely for victory, which is seldom conceded, but which, if even by general consent achieved, is too often connected with alienation of feeling and the excitement of bitter animosities in the minds of partisans on both sides. Men do not enter into controversy with the desire to ascertain the truth. Each steps into the arena with a conviction, not to be shaken, that he is the champion of the truth; and having taken his stand, he feels it incumbent upon him to sustain not only his opinions, but himself. Whoever heard of a controversialist that acknowledged himself to be convinced of error and that openly yielded to the force of his antagonist's arguments? True, those who, not being committed to either party, dispassionately witness the contest may be aided in the acquisition of truth; but with the combatants and their friends, the more ordinary result is that they are each more firmly established in their respective sentiments. To a man of pacific temper, therefore, it is disagreeable to engage in controversy, and the earnest seeker after truth will more easily attain to it by any other process. But yet, religious controversy is sometimes necessary. The world abounds in errors, and we are commanded to contend and earnestly, too, for the faith once delivered to the saints.

Assaults upon truth committed to our trust should be met, whatever may be the character of the assailant, and whatever the manner in which he conducts his assaults. True, it is always more agreeable, and sometimes more consonant with one's self-respect, to pass by in silence the dogmatic and the uncandid; but necessity requires, however much our disgust may be excited, that we notice even them, otherwise they may be wise in their own conceits, and the wavering may have misgivings that their attacks cannot be repelled. In engaging in controversy with persons of this description, however, we should see to it that we are influenced solely by a regard for the truth, and that we be not provoked into the same unlovely spirit which they betray. It is always an evidence of an unsanctified temper, or of the weakness of our cause or of both, when we indulge in personalities and abuse. Never until we feel that our arguments are exhausted are we tempted to stand by our arms. The weapons of the Christian's warfare should never be carnal, and his self-respect as a gentleman should make him scorn to bandy epithets with an antagonist. Not that we would be understood to say that a Christian should never use severity. It is often as necessary to answer the man as the argument; and in doing so, rebuke administered with a proper spirit and in a proper manner, exerts sometimes a wholesome influence.

Thus much would we say, partly in deprecation of the necessity which seems to impel us to controvert the positions of the publication whose title we have given above, and partly as an assertion of the principles by which we shall be governed in the attempt.

This is a pamphlet of twenty-eight pages and contains the substance of two sermons delivered in various parts of Middle Georgia in 1849. They created quite a sensation at the time, and their author, having no further use for them for the pulpit, has slightly expurgated them, and the world is now blessed with them in a more permanent form. They are designed as attacks (in their author's opinion, it would seem, very effective ones) upon the Calvinistic doctrines of Predestination and, what is called, the Final Perseverance of the Saints. There is nothing original about them, excepting the spirit that is exhibited and some ingenious misapprehensions of the plain language of Calvinistic writers, which no one before has been so constituted as to fall into. Leaving these out of view, the remaining is made up of arguments in a diluted state, borrowed, without acknowledgment, from standard Arminian writers; and if we were assured that our readers are in

18

possession of the authors on the Calvinistic side of the question, we should consider our's (excepting in so far as we may be performing a service to our author) a work of supererogation. This publication, we suppose, is but an earnest of what is to follow as we are told on page 1: "We are determined that if it (Calvinism) lives any longer than we do that it shall not be our fault." We hope that on this announcement, our Calvinistic readers will not give way to unnecessary alarm: Calvinism had survived Arminius, and Whitby, and Wesley, and Fletcher, and Watson, and a host of other able assailants. Let us live in hopes, therefore, that it may possibly survive even Mr. Reneau.

Our author, however, has formally declared war against Calvinism and, in effect, announced that he has not only drawn his sword but thrown the scabbard away. The war, under his direction, is to be of the most sanguinary character. Nothing short of complete extermination will satisfy him. "We have determined that if it (Calvinism) lives any longer than we do that it shall not be our fault." No quarter is to be granted - perhaps none is to be asked. Conscious of his strength, he may be confident that he will occupy the victorious position of Samson when in triumph he sung: "With the jaw of an ass have I slain a thousand men;" or perhaps, like the same Samson in adversity, he anticipates that, by a mighty effort of strength, he will rejoice to overwhelm in one common destruction both himself and his enemies. However this may be, we confess it shocks us to hear such a blood-thirsty determination announced. There are to be granted no terms of honorable capitulation - the forces of Calvinism are not to be cheered with the hope that, if it come to the worst, they can save their lives by surrendering at discretion. Entreat as piteously as they may for mercy, it is in no case to be granted them. The life-blood of one or both, it is sternly decided, must water the ground! Is not this the nineteenth century? Has not the savage ferocity of war been mitigated by the spirit of the Gospel and by the humanizing influences of advancing civilization? We hope our author, for his own sake, will reconsider this determination. It may make Calvinism desperate. If he has no bowels of mercy and no respect for "the spirit of the age," - if none of the softer or the nobler motives can influence him, then let prudence and sound policy cause him to haul down that blood-red flag. If he has unrelentingly determined that the forces of Calvinism shall, in no case, be prisoners on parole, let them have the consolation to know that they shall be prisoners of some sort, or they will sell their lives as dearly as possible.

But, after all, we are more than half inclined to think that the danger to Calvinism from him has its existence only in our author's harmless self-complacency. That he considers himself a warrior of no inferior stamp - destined to achieve victories which no polemical hero before him (he tacitly acknowledges) has been adequate to, is abundantly evident, not only from this, but from other passages of his production; but we see no reason why any body else should labor under the same delusion - surely there is none to be found in the performance before us. It is no uncommon thing for men to "think of themselves more highly than they ought to think." Where they are composed of materials suitable for the purpose and placed in a favorable position, a very little encouragement makes them in fancy swell out beyond all reasonable proportions: and there is no conception of themselves too exalted for them to entertain. Herod, while listening to the adulation of his courtiers, fancied himself a God; and a wise King of Macedon, aware of his propensity of poor human nature, enjoined it upon one of his household to repeat to him daily, "Remember, O King, that thou art mortal!" We are not quite sure that a monitor of the same kind would not be of service to our author?

Notwithstanding, however, he broadly intimates that he has much confidence in his success, his language would seem to imply that he has some apprehension that he may, after all, fail in his super-human enterprise. "If it lives any longer than we do, it shall not be our fault." He will at least make a conscientious use of the strength he possesses. He feels that a solemn responsiblity rests upon him in the premises - that much has been given him and therefore much will be required of him. The blood of all the controversialists flows through his veins - the strength of all the champions of Arminianism nerves his arm" - "his height is six cubits and a span" (I Sam. 17:4), and he is commanded to use his resources for the annihilation of Calvinism. Will he come up to his responsibilities? If he fails it shall not be his fault! But suppose Calvinism should not be accommodating enough to die when he attacks it, how will he infallibly know that he has acquitted himself as in duty bound? We fancy that we see him now harassed by the most painful uncertainty. Some months ago he made his first attack and discharged at his enemy seventy-two paragraphs (all numbered off), and since then silence has reigned over the field of operations. If he fancies that this silence is caused by his complete success and that Calvinism lies among the slain, it becomes our painful office to inform him that it is not dead but sleepeth and that we are the only one of its friends that seem to have been awakened by the noise of the attack! But then what becomes of his conscientious determination so to act as to avoid blame? Could he not have hurled one paragraph more? Did he have no other shot to fire? Perhaps another shot, more lucky than the rest, might have reached his enemy's heart and freed the world of bondage. Why then did he not discharge it? If he did all that he could, what becomes of his ostentatious profession of strength? Verily there seems to be an antagonism here - Strength vs. Conscience. His exalted conceptions of himself, or his conscience, one or the other, must give way. Our author's estimate of his powers must be lowered, in the present aspect of the case, or (his conscience remaining lively) he must be in the most painful state of uncertainty as to whether he is to be any longer responsible for the existence of Calvinism. Verily, Atlas requires much strength to sustain the weight of the world!

"I am determined, that if it survives my attacks!" Surely Mr. Reneau's perception of the ludicrous must be defective? Calvinism has never heard of him before, and if its advocates ever think of him hereafter, it will never be in a connection flattering to his vanity!

We confidently believe that no publication in the language of the same length, contains as great an amount of bitterness and as many examples of misrepresentation as that upon which we are animadverting. The author seems to have written with the feelings of the man, who having the most self-satisfying confidence in his own prowess, and having ostentatiously called upon the whole world to witness the ease with which he would demolish his antagonist, is made conscious at last of a disgraceful failure, and vents his impotent rage by abusive epithets at a respectful distance. Like the Mexican Chief, who soothed the mortification of repulse by pronouncing the American General so ignorant of military science as not to know when he was defeated - or, more properly, like the blustering quallelsome urchin, who said if he could not chastise the larger boy he could make faces at him.

The following examples of his style and spirit, under appropriate heads, are given, not because they are the worst of their kind, but because they are shorter and can be more easily extracted.

His Courtesy and Liberality. - "But in order to carry out their Calvinistic scheme, this talk, &c., has been made a part of their visionary scheme and theories;" - "To exhibit still further the mad scheme of this system," &c., p.16. "No man that prefers the truth to his own prejudices, it would seem to us, could doubt that Jesus did intend on this occasion to teach that his disciples might lose their religion." "Calvinists holding on to their error with a zeal worthy of a better cause." - "if we were to admit this foolish hypothesis." p.19. "No man can mistake here provided his prejudices have not blinded him and so wholly perverted his understanding, that nothing could instruct him." p.21. "Is there a man on this Camp-Ground stupid enough to believe such to be the true meaning of these texts of Holy Writ? Every one who has sense enough to know the road to the mill knows better." p.23. "We feel that enough has been said to satisfy every honest enquirer after truth, that it is possible for a man to receive the grace of God in vain and thus perish everlastingly." p.23. "Do Calvinists think the world dull enough to believe that such argument makes out their doctrine?" p.27.

His CANDOR. - "It is palpable that Calvinists hold that God's elect are ordained to everlasting life without any regard to their Christian character." p. 14

His DOGMATISM. — "This is indeed a very convenient method of proving an unscriptural doctrine." p.6. "If we believe no more concerning predestination than the Bible teaches, we will never believe the Calvinistic notion on that subject." p.11. "Neither these" (passages of scripture) "nor any others prove anything at all in their favor." p.27.

His REFINEMENT. — "If a poor reprobate were to commit such crimes, eternal damnation in Hell-fire would be the consequence, but let one of these predestinated pets commit them, and they will have the headache or some other punishment and then bask in heaven's smiles world without end." p.15.

Any where else than in a sermon, this would be called slang. Other examples under this head we deem it proper to suppress, as they are too gross to meet the eye of our lady readers.

His DEFERENCE TO THE BIBLE. - "Convince us that Christianity tolerates such things, and we will plead its cause no more." p.15.

Finally, in the way of extracts: "We fear our Calvinistic friends will not easily forgive us for our frank dealing with their favorite doctrines." p.17. "If our Calvinistic brethren feel hurt, they may rest assured that we deliver these sentiments out of no unkind feelings. It is because we thus believe that we thus preach." p.12. We hope that after this none of our Calvinistic readers will be so unreasonable as to continue dissatisfied. True, our author says that they are "silly" and "dull" and "stupid" and "prejudiced" and "dishonest" and "without sense enough to know the road to the mill", but "it is because he thus believes that he thus writes." Let us, therefore, be grateful for his tenderness and repress our complainings.

The Bible addresses us in plain and intelligible language. While there are many mysteries in it that angels desire in vain to look into and many things difficult to be understood which the perverse frequently wrest to their own destruction, those truths which pertain to eternal life are revealed in the most unambiguous language. God does not dishonor Himself and trifle with His creatures by making their salvation to depend upon the reception of doctrines that are either unintelligible or contradictory. His system of heavenly truth is harmonious and consistent; and revealed with perspicuity and precision. Commencing here on earth with the first "principles of the doctrine of Christ" - with "repentance from dead works and faith toward God," it ascends a glorious chain, each link shining more brightly as it rises into the pure heavens above until it glitters in the effulgence that shines from God's throne. We are not only commanded to search the scriptures, but we are encouraged by the promise that we shall know if we follow on to know the Lord. Like his sanctification, the path of the Christian's knowledge is as the shining light that shines more and more unto the perfect day. God designed that His people should understand His truth - nay, He has made their salvation to depend upon their belief of it - and it is His will that they should all come into the unity of the faith, that they should be one as Christ and the Father are one. Why then is there such a diversity of sentiment in the Christian world? Why is it that even evangelical sects draw from the scriptures systems so diametrically opposite? That good men do differ in theological sentiment is indisputable and is as lamentable as it is true; but the reason is not to be found in any ambiguity in the word of God. Some of the difference, perhaps, is to be ascribed to the diversity of their mental constitution and the different way in which the same evidence strikes different minds; much to the force of early bias, to the influence of association, and to the distorted media, therefore through which the truth is seen - much to the carelessness with which many read the scriptures and to the indolence which causes them to construct a system out of fragments of Bible truth; but without doubt no inconsiderable part of the disagreement is to be attributed to presumption. Professing Christians (sometimes unconsciously) not infrequently form in advance an idea in their minds - drawn from the teachings of others or from their own reflections - of the character of God and of the doctrines which he ought to promulgate and then afterwards consult the Bible to prove that their views are correct; and some carry their presumption to such daring lengths as to reject the Bible if it fails to sustain them in their positions. May not those opinions, which would rob Christ of His divinity, which deny the doctrine of the trinity - and those others which would make eternal life the portion of all mankind, have their origin here?

While we are far from the bigotry which would make us assert that the denomination to which we belong are the only people exempt from this presumption, and as far from the illiberality which would induce us to apply it to any individual who may differ from us - while we are free to grant, until evidence appear to the contrary, that all evangelical Christians who differ from us are as honest seekers after truth as we are; we feel no hesitation in placing any one in this category who openly confesses it to be his appropriate place. Such our author has done. He has, in effect, declared that, if it can be shown to him that the Bible teaches Calvinism, he will reject it, and turn his back upon it. "Convince us that Christianity tolerates such things, and we will plead its cause no more." p.15. Like the madman in "The World's Anti-slavery Convention" who said: convince me that the Bible sanctions slavery, and I cast it to the winds and learn my religion from the flowers of the field. The "things" he refers to here are such as he ascribes - it matters not whether justly or unjustly - to Calvinists, and which do not therefore, by universal consent, bear upon their face the infallible marks of falsity. Convince him that the sentiments of Edwards, and Doddridge, and Baxter, and a host of other worthies - who lived in the faith, and who being dead yet speak - are tolerated by the word of God, and he will plead its cause no more! Verily he has placed himself in a dilemma from which it is impossible that he can be extricated. If he knew in his heart that these sentiments, which were so horrifying to him, were no less decidedly rejected by all other Christians, and that he could therefore with safety stake his reverence for the Bible upon their falsity, then he was guilty of bearing false witness against his brethren. But if he sincerely believed that they were the sentiments of his opponents, then he stands convicted of prescribing terms to Almighty God and of saying to Him that if it can be proved that He sanctions Calvinism, he will plead His cause no more!

He utters a threat that, in a certain contingency mentioned, he "will plead the cause of Christianity no more." It is evidently his intention here that somebody should take warning - But who? Not his opponents, surely; for if their measure of his efficiency come up to the half his pretensions, they would rejoice that there is a prospect of his quitting the field: not his friends and co-laborers; for they are innocent of any blame in the premises. Against whom then is the threat uttered? Is it possible that our author is unconscious of its impious nature!

The advocates of Calvinism seem to be in a strait here betwixt two. If they permit the argument to go against them by default, they give up what they conceive to be important scripture truth: if they vanquish their assailant, they do it at the expense of making an infidel of him - or we should rather say, of driving him into open connection with infidels; for his threat contains already all the essential elements of infidelity. No explanation can make it much better for him, but we would fain hope, that this sentence escaped him in the heat of chronic passion!

And this is the man that with so much confidence intimates that he is destined to exterminate Calvinism from the land! How will he do it? He has fallen upon a poor expedient to prepare the way for success. We thank God that, in this highly favored land, the doctrine of the Reformation so generally prevails: "The Bible, without note or comment, the only and the all sufficient rule of faith and practice." The people profess to yield themselves with humble submission to the teachings of God's word, and they will say to him and to all others like him, "Let God be true, but every man a liar."

It is a rule in parliamentary proceedings that if the provisions of a bill do not conform to its title, it is to be rejected. Were our author's first sermon tried by the same principle, it would meet with the same fate. It has seldom been our lot to read a production (as far as the argument is concerned) so desultory and incongrous. He uses his arguments in as arbitrary a manner as he does the figures with which he begins his paragraphs. Question them as closely as you may, you will fail to learn from them their adaptation to the case in hand. Old as they are and as much as they have seen of the world, we venture the assertion they have never found themselves in such strange connections before. What dependence they have upon each other and what support they mutually afford, it is difficult to discern. And yet they need all the assistance they can obtain; for, divest them of the martial livery put upon them by their present owner and exorcise them of the evil spirit with which they are possessed, and they are exhibited to be of the most feeble and attentuated nature with hardly strength enough to maintain a perpendicular attitude Besides, being employed from their youth for other purposes now that old age and hard usage are added to constitutional weakness, they do not possess the flexibility which would make them useful auxiliaries in an employment so contrary to their natures and their habits. Never, perhaps, were very innocent arguments so badly treated. Another example, doubtless, tending to establish the truth of the old saying - that we esteem that lightly which cost us little.

But, we have said that the production is desultory and incongrous. In the title, the author proposes to attack Calvinistic Predestination; but, in giving a description of it, he defines (in a lame and ungrammatical way) Election; while the attack itself is leveled chiefly at the doctrine of necessity, as opposed to the Arminian idea of Liberty or self-determining power! Why is this? Is it because he is ignorant of that which he professes to assail; or, aping a skillful General, does he design to weaken the point aimed at, by compelling the garrison (as expecting a general attack) to occupy, at the same time, the whole line of defence? Does he amuse us with feigned attacks, that he may mask his real intentions? If so, we submit to him whether this comports with the confidence, more than hinted, that his forces are sufficient, by dint of mere strength, to raze our fortress to its foundations and to put the garrison to the sword? And it may be well, too, for him to bear in mind that, while deceptions on a warlike theatre and on a large scale are called by dignified names and, when successful, are applauded in a more limited sphere, they degenerate into mere tricks which not infrequently bring their perpetrators into merited contempt.

Election and the doctrine of Necessity are important parts of Predestination, but they do not constitute the whole of it. Why, then, did he not give to his readers a definition of Predestination in the very words of its advocates and attempt, fairly and in a manly way, a refutation of it in all its parts and as a whole? Only two suppositions can be given. Either he did not comprehend that to which he was objecting, or he designedly left it in uncertainty that he might avail himself of all the prejudices and misapprehensions of his hearers - that, by using disjoined parts (and disfigured at that) of the Calvinistic system, united with others of his own invention, he might construct a hideous image (adapting it to his capacity as an adversary) and call it Predestination; and, having demolished this, his depraved creature (to the relief of Calvinists, no less than of Arminians) might set up a shout of triumph, as if he had gained a victory over Calvinism. This course may have been very successful (on a small scale) for the time; but our author will find that it will re-act, with retributive force upon himself. He may have thought, while skipping about, with such marvellous agility over all parts of the field (excepting the right one) - making so much noise and raising such a smoke - that he would bewilder his adversary and gain the admiration of the lookers-on; and, if he should fail of victory, find at least in the smoke and dust a concealment from the resentment he provoked. But let him know that Calvinism, if it feel so disposed, can trace him out in the deep obscurity he has created, and, having dragged him forth into the light, can bestow upon him before the world the chastisement which will be salutary, not only for his correction, but as a warning to all like him inclined.

Our author possesses some of that ingenuity which is efficient in misrepresenting an opponent and is gifted in no ordinary degree with the powers of denunciation and abuse; but he seems to be entirely destitute of analysis. We defy any one to extract a complete skeleton from this sermon. It would seem as if he sat down to write, without any system in his mind, and with nothing to guide his ideas but the bitter feelings by which they were impelled. The only difficulties, therefore, in the way of answering his arguments consist 1st - in finding out what they are, and 2nd - in perceiving what bearing they have upon the subject after they are discovered. In his title, he essays to give us a treatise on Predestination; but, excepting the arbitrary use of the word, his denunciation is of any other Calvinistic doctrine rather.

Amphora coepit
Institui; currente rota cur urceus exit?

Again, he professes to treat of Calvinistic doctrines; but, in his statement of them, he quotes from the writings of Dr. Hopkins! Now, every polemic theologian ought to know that the Doctor was the founder of a distinct school and is not acknowledged as a Calvinist at all. Many of his sentiments, doubtless, as well as those of James Arminius, conform to our system; but this makes the one, not more than the other, a disciple of John Calvin. Why, then, is Dr. Hopkins cited in this connection? If he meant not to violate the common principles of fairness, he furnishes us with another instance of his inability to pursue steadily the object before him. Having a grudge against the Calvinists, he belabors the Hopkinsains! Let him take care lest he may by mistake kill the wrong man. That would be very sad and may be, if possible, a source of regret even to him. But, why did he not quote from those exclusively who are universally acknowledged as standard Calvinistic writers? To have done so would have given him less opportunity perhaps for the exercise of his peculiar gifts; but it would have been more candid, and we will say also more manly. It matters not though the language quoted from Dr. Hopkins expressed exactly Calvinistic sentiments; it is enough to know that we are no more responsible for him than we are for Mr. Reneau. And this is another specimen of his candor! It would seem that he is so bent on the destruction of Calvinism as to feel authorized for this purpose to adopt the Roman Catholic principle that the end sanctifies the means. This, however, is not one of the most glaring of the misrepresentations with which his pamphlet abounds. We do not know that it will be of any avail; but we would advise him, hereafter, to take pains in advance to understand any thing before he attacks it and to endeavor to treat his opponents with justice and candor. It may make him feel better and fare better - "All they that take the sword shall perish with the sword."

SECTION II

It would be a sufficient defense of Predestination against our author, to show that, notwithstanding his professions, he does not attack it at all; but, as he seems to look upon his arguments with much complacency and the task is to us not destitute of entertainment, we waive this method of defense, and engage to ramble about with him, and to sustain any Calvinistic doctrines he may have attacked, whether designedly or by mistake. As we essay to answer Mr. Reneau, we must meet him where he is, since we cannot find him where he ought to be. Before doing so, however, we seem it proper to state the much abused doctrine of Predestination. We are the more inclined to do so, as we have reason to believe that our author is not the only one who entertains confused notions in regard to it.

"Predestination is that eternal, most wise, and immutable decrcc of God, whereby he did, form before all

28

time, determined and ordain to create, dispose of, and direct to some particular end, every person and thing to which he has given, or is yet to give, being; and to make the whole creation subservient to, and declarative of, his own glory." "The Lord hath made all things for himself: yea, even the wicked for the day of evil" (Prov. 16:4) - Zanchius

The doctrine, as we think, necessarily grows out of the character of God, and his connection with the universe as its creator, upholder, and governor.

The following series of propositions, analytically disposed, contains, as we conceive, both the statement, and the proof of it:

1. This earth was created by God, and, consequently, there was a period when it began to exist.

2. God created it not of necessity, or from impulse, but according to the good pleasure of His will, and as the result of a settled purpose entertained from eternity.

3. As an infinitely wise and reasonable being, he had some ultimate object, well-defined, and specific, which he proposed to attain by its creation (Prov. 16:4; Rom. 11:36; Rev. 4:11).

4. Possessing infinite knowledge, he knew, by intuition not only all things that have existed, and shall exist, but all things possible - "all possible causes, and all their possible effects" (Ps. 147:5; I Sam. 23:11, 12; Mt. 11:21, 23). Therefore, out of an endless diversity of worlds comprehended in the divine knowledge as possible, he selected such an one as this - composed as it is, and peopled as it is, - as the most suitable means for the accomplishment of his purpose: and decreed that it should exist (Col. 1:16).

5. That this ultimate object might be attained, and the end infallibly secured, he ordained, with unerring certainty, all the means necessary, both in the world of matter, and in the world of mind. He not only fixed, from eternity, all the forms, positions, relations, and motions of matter, even to the numbering of the hairs of our heads, and deciding when a sparrow should fall - in directing the motions of the particles of dust in the atmosphere, (Isa. 40:12) and ordaining when the sun should shine, (Job 9:7) and when the wind should blow, (Ps.135:7), but he "fixed from eternity all the circumstances in the life of every individual or mankind and all the particulars which will compose the history of the human race from its commencement to its close."

6. God's foreknowledge relates to those things that should occur in time; and he foreknew, therefore, that those would occur rather than the other innumerable things that were

possible, because he had decreed that they, and not others, should exist. (Eph. 1:11; Acts 15:18; Ps. 115:6; Acts 17:26).

7. The world, therefore, in all its physical and moral details, is just as God designed it to be - the entrance of moral evil itself not excepted. He did not err in his plan, therefore evil did not enter unexpectedly to him - he has not been frustrated in his purpose, therefore it did not enter in spite of him. And this too is in perfect consistency with the declaration of scripture, that God is not the author of sin.

1. God is not only the creator but the upholder of all things (Heb. 1:3). In him we live, and move, and have our being. He not only bestowed upon men their faculties, but He gives them the ability to use them. He preserves those powers when they are employed in opposition to him, no less than when they are employed in his service.

2. This he does not from a choice of evils, i.e. not because he is compelled, by the force of circumstances, which he cannot control, to take this as an evil rather than some other that is greater, for, possessing almighty power, he might have paralyzed those faculties, or prevented their abuse by changing the hearts of their owners.

3. Possessing infallible prescience, he foresaw all the instances in which ungodly men would sin against him; and, permitting it in time, he determined to permit it from all eternity, and decreeing from eternity to permit it, it entered into his plan, and composed a part of the purpose which he entertained before the world was.

1. God, as the governor of the world, administers all things according to his sovereign pleasure. He doeth according to his will in the army of heaven, and among the inhabitants of the earth; and none can stay his hand, or say unto him, What doest thou?

2. "He did not merely decree that general laws should be established for the government of the world, but he settled the application of those laws to all particular cases." Our days are numbered, and so are the hairs of our heads. His providence takes cognizance of, and controls everything however minute (Ps. 135:6; Acts 17:25, 26, 28; Matt. 6:26, 30, &c). "It upholds, directs, disposes, and governs all creatures, actions and things, from the greatest even to the least."

3. Now, as known unto God are all his works from the beginning of the world, and, as he is immutable in his nature, it follows that what he does in time he determined to do from eternity - that his providence is but the enforcement of those laws and the revealment of those plans, which existed before

the world was. Finally, it follows that "whatever occurs in time was fore-ordained before the beginning of time."

In reference to men, predestination is divided into two parts: 1st - as it relates to the elect, and 2nd - as it relates to the non-elect. Having decreed to create a world and to people it with beings who would voluntarily sin against him, he determined from eternity to save some and to leave others to perish in their sins. "Willing to show his wrath and to make his power known," he "endured with much long suffering" these as "the vessels of wrath fitted to destruction: and that he might make known the riches of his glory on" those as "the vessels of mercy which he had afore prepared unto glory" (Rom. 9:22-23).

To carry out his purpose of grace, he chose some to holiness and eternal life, entered for their sake into the Covenant of Redemption with the Son and the Holy Ghost, appointed his Son as their substitute, to suffer in their stead, and, having died, to rise again and appear as their advocate before his throne, appointed all the intermediate means necessary and, by an infallible decree, made their salvation sure. Those "whose names are not written in the book of life" (Rev. 20:15), who are "appointed to wrath" (I Thes. 5:9), who were "before of old ordained to condemnation" (Jude 4), who would "stumble at the word, being disobedient, whereunto also they were appointed" (I Pet. 2:8), he determined to leave in their sins and to endure them with much long suffering as vessels of wrath fitted to destruction.

The elect are chosen, not because God foresees faith and good works in them; but in part that they might have faith and might perform good works; or, in the language of the Confession of Faith, quoted by our author: "God hath chosen them in Christ, unto everlasting glory, out of his mere free grace and love, without any foresight of faith or good works, or perseverance in either of them, or any other thing in the creature, as conditions, or causes moving him thereunto." God's act in electing some and not others is to be resolved into his sovereign will. He hath mercy on whom he will have mercy, and whom he will he hardeneth (Rom. 9:18).

While, by an immutable decree, He has made all things in time fixed and sure, all this occurs in perfect consistency with the free agency of the creature, and God is not the author of sin. The elect are, by the influence of sovereign grace, made willing in the day of God's power and those not elected have no active principle of disobedience imparted to them, and feel no restraint upon their wills - they are simply passed by, and permitted to follow the inclinations of their own hearts. While they work out God's purposes, they do it unconsciously and wickedly. "Him (Christ) being delivered by the determinate counsel and foreknowledge of God, ye have taken and by wicked hands have crucified and slain" (Acts 2:23).

REMARK 1. Whatever objections may be raised against this doctrine (and what doctrine is there against which objections cannot be raised) can be shown to press with greater weight upon the Arminian system.

REMARK 2. Much of the difficulty in the way of the reception of this doctrine grows out of the two following considerations:

1. We are too much disposed to think of the eternal God as if He were just such a being as we are. Looking too exclusively upon our free agency and accountability, we lose sight of God's sovereignty and omniscience. Confining our observations only to the brief period which limits our existence on earth, we view Him as a mere contemporary with ourselves whose only jurisdiction is to reward us if we do well, to note our improper conduct if we act amiss, and to bring us into judgment hereafter. It does not enter into our conceptions that He existed from all eternity and, as our Creator, has supreme ownership of us - that He was under no obligation to create us nor to destine us for one end rather than another. Our pride and self-love cause us to rebel at the declaration that God, in making and in disposing of us, consults His sovereign pleasure and His glory rather than our interests. And we are disposed to reply against God. As if He had not, in the beginning, in reference to us, the same right and the same power that the potter has out of clay to make one vessel unto honor and another unto dishonor (Rom. 9:21).

2. Another cause of hesitation to receive this doctrine springs from a desire to avoid any belief which seems dishonoring to God. Taking a partial and superficial (and sometimes distorted) view of the subject, some consider it to be inconsistent with His goodness and impartiality to decree to save some and to leave others to perish in their sins. But let them take care while they quarrel with what God decrees that they do not quarrel with what He does. It is evident that all men are not saved, and that those that are, are saved by the operations of His grace. Now, if it is consistent with God's honor to save some in time and to leave others to perish in their sins, it is consistent with it to decree to do so from eternity.

Besides, supposing we grant that there were no divine decrees, we see not how the difficulty is obviated. God knew before He created them and from eternity who would reject the gospel and finally perish, and yet He gave them being notwithstanding - though He was under no necessity to do so. He might have created them with dispostions to do His will, or He might have not created them at all. Is He not as much responsible for the destruction of the wicked on the one supposition as on the other? As much on the Arminian principle as on the Calvinistic? God knows better than we do what is consistent with His character and how to preserve His honor - we shall be perfectly safe, therefore, in believing implicitly all that He reveals on the subject. And this is His testimony: "The Lord of hosts hath sworn, (i.e. has immutably decreed) saying, Surely as I have thought, so shall it come to pass: and as I have purposed, so shall it stand. This is the purpose that is purposed upon the whole earth; and this is the hand that is stretched out upon all the nations. For the Lord of hosts hath purposed, and who shall disannul it? and his hand is stretched out, and who shall turn it back?"(Is.14:24,26,27).

In the above, we have given a statement of Predestination in such terms as we think to carry the proof along with it; but as it is an eminently practical doctrine and one much caviled at, we proceed to argue its truth by starting from a different point. Be it remembered, however, that Mr. Reneau has laid us under no obligation to take this course nor, indeed, to have said any thing on Predestination proper. As it is, therefore, a mere gratuity to him, we hope he will not be insensible of the favor - though, as his organs are weak, we are not sure that it may not prove too hard for him to digest. Indeed, it would not be surprising if it should turn out a file which he cannot bite.

That God, from all eternity, ordained all things that should occur in time both in the world of matter and in the world of mind will follow, as an inevitable conclusion, if we shall be able to establish the following premises:

Position 1. God has intimate relations with all the works of His hands. This, we suppose, none of our readers will deny. No one entertains the Epicurian notion that God, after creating the world, and ordaining general physical laws for its government; withdrew into some distant part of His universe and since then has taken no cognizance of His creatures. Nor does any one believe that He is a mere unconcerned spectator of the actions and events that transpire in this lower world. He fills immensity with His presence and maintains intimate personal relations with all the works of His hands:

1st. He upholds all things by the word of His power (Heb. 1:3). We suppose it susceptible of demonstration, were it necessary, that it requires as great an exertion of almighty power to preserve, as originally to have called into existence, the universe; and that, if His upholding and sustaining power were removed, it would instantly fall back into the nothingness from whence it sprang. By Him, all inanimate matter, in the aggregate, and, therefore, in its minutest parts is preserved. In Him, the tallest Archangel and the most degraded descendant of Adam, live and move and have their being. "Thou hast made heaven, the heaven of heavens, with all their host, the earth, with all things that are therein, the seas, and all that is therein, and thou preservest them all" (Neh. 9:6).

2nd. God provides for all His creatures - Whether directly or through the agency of second causes (which he controls), He gives to all His living creatures their meat in due season (Ps. 104:27). To men, He gives rain from heaven and fruitful seasons, filling their hearts with food and gladness (Acts 14:17) and commands His people to pray to Him daily: Give us this day our daily bread. He opens His hand and satisfies the desire of every living thing (Ps. 145:16), gives to the beast his food and to the young ravens which cry (Ps. 147:9), feeds the fowls of the air (Mt. 6:26), and, in a word, giveth food to all flesh (Ps. 136:25).

3rd. God disposes and governs all His creatures. He appointed the limits to the land and said to the sea, Hitherto shalt thou come and no further; and here shall thy proud waves be stayed (Job 38:11). He gathered together in heaps those particles of earth that form the mountains, and he strewed the grains of sand that form the sea shore - giving to each one its allotted place. His hand keeps on their firm foundations the everlasting hills, and He disposes every particle of dust: by His direction, they float through the atmosphere or settle in the position to which His hand guides them (Is. 40:12). He scooped out the channels through which mighty rivers flow and sent the springs to run through the valleys (Ps. 104:10) - marking out all their sinuosities, directing all their mutations, and guiding all the watery particles that, from time to time, unite to replenish their failing waters. By His direction, some particles of moisture flow towards the sea and some, ascending in vapor, form clouds. By His appointment, they descend in genial showers to fertilize the fields, or in torrents causing the channels of the rivers to overflow and bearing destruction to property and to life. The elements are ruled by Him (Job 37: 9-13; Is. 50:2; Jn. 1:4,15; Neh. 1:4). He covereth the heavens with clouds; He prepareth rain for the earth; He giveth snow like wool; He scattereth the hoar frost like ashes; He casteth forth His ice like morsels. Who can stand before His cold? He sendeth out His word and melteth them; He causeth His winds to blow and the waters to flow (Ps. 147:8,16-18). In no less sovereign way does He dispose of His creature, man. He decides when he shall be born, and where, and of what parents, though the most momentous consequences attend upon the decision. By His appointment, some come into existence in the midst of a heathen community, where their whole lives are spent without an opportunity to hear of the God of the Bible or to learn the way of salvation through Christ. While, to others, their lives are cast by Him in pleasant places. They are nurtured, by His appointment, in a community in whose midst Christ Jesus is permanently set forth - evidently crucified among them. Some, He makes the offspring of ungodly parents, who rear them up in irreligion and vice and teach them to blaspheme His Name and to despise His authority; while others are descended from a long line of pious ancestry - are raised up in the nurture and admonition of the Lord and, like Timothy, have from their childhood the Holy Scriptures, which are able to make them wise unto eternal life. He ordains all the worldly circumstances and conditions of men. However wise their plans and strenuous their exertions, without the blessing of the Lord upon their efforts, they fail of success. "The Lord maketh poor and maketh rich; He bringeth low, and lifteth up. He raiseth up the poor out of the dust, and lifteth up the beggar from the dunghill, to set them among princes, and to make them inherit the throne of glory" (I Sam. 2:7,8; with Ps. 75:67). The ways of men are ordered by Him. However conscious they may be of their independence - that they are acting freely and following the bent of their own inclinations - an unseen power controls them in all their ways. "A man's heart deviseth his way; but the Lord directeth his steps" (Prov. 16:9). "There are many devices in a man's heart; nevertheless, the counsel of the Lord that shall stand (Prov. 19:21, with 20:24). They have no right to say: Today or tomorrow we will do thus and so; but: If the Lord will, we shall live and do this or that (Ja. 4:15). He holds, with a firm grasp, the reins of dominion over His creatures and worketh all things after the counsel of His own will (Eph. 1:11). All causes and all effects, in the material world, obey His command, and all the antecedents and consequents in the immaterial, He controls. The preparation of the heart and the answer of the tongue is with the Lord. He works in his obedient subjects to will and to do of His good pleasure; and the disobedient sin against Him,

He not hindering - not, however, in spite of His power (John 19:11); and, in doing so, they accomplish ulterior objects that he has in view (Gen. 50:20; Is. 10:6,7,12; Rom. 9:17; II Sam. 24:1,10, with I Chron. 21:1; Acts 4:27,28). God determines the period of human life (Ps. 31:15, 39:5; Acts 17:26). The days of all the descendants of Adam are numbered. Various are the terms allotted to individuals; but the times of all are in His hand (Ps. 31:15). Some, in early youth, are hurried in impenitency from time to eternity; while others, more favored, are spared to make their peace with God when their heads are frosted with age. In a word, God is nigh to every one of us, and His providence ruleth over all. Whatsoever the Lord pleased, that did He in heaven and in earth, in the seas, and all deep places (Ps. 135:6). As an upholder, a provider, a disposer, and a governor, God maintains the most intimate relations with all the works of His hands.

Position 2. In all these relations with His creatures, God governs Himself by a determinate plan. To deny this is to rob Him of intelligence and wisdom. Even a wise man who has a valuable object to attain or is engaged in some important enterprise lays down a well-digested plan of operations and establishes those rules to govern his exertions which, in his opinion, will be most likely to insure him success. A skillful General marks out the plan of his campaigns; a farmer, a plan by which to cultivate his estate; a statesman, a plan by which to administer the affairs of the government; and so on to the end of the chapter. It is a mark of stupidity and of folly among men to attempt any thing without system and to expect to attain great results by impulse and at haphazard. God, therefore, who possesses the attributes of wisdom and intelligence in an infinite degree knows what he intends and what will most infallibly secure that result. Now while it is not necessary for Him to make an array of forces so as to overcome obstacles in the way of the attainment of His results - while it is only necessary for Him to speak and it is done, to command and it stands fast - yet, as an infinitely wise Being, He knows the ends He proposes and the best means for the attainment of those ends: and these means He selects; and these means, selected constitute His plan. Again - When time shall be no more and the history of God's actions towards His creatures shall be complete, the aggregate of those actions will constitute a system. Now, this system of actions, as a whole and in all its parts, is such as God designs it to be - or it is not. If not, then God acts fortuitously and impulsively without any definite object and at random. If it is, then He governs Himself in all these actions by a determinate plan which infinite wisdom devised. God works all things after the counsel of His will. Our God is in the heavens; He hath done whatsoever He pleased (Ps. 115:3).

Position 3. This determinate plan existed from all eternity. This follows from the infinite perfections of His nature - from His immutability. If He has a plan in time which He had not in eternity, then His mind has undergone a change. But, He says: I am the Lord - I change not (Mal. 3:6). He is the same yesterday, today, and forever, without variableness or shadow of turning - from His infinite knowledge. If a plan exists in the Divine Mind, it is designed either to produce the occurances in time or to meet them: either it is the cause of events or is caused by them. Upon either supposition, it existed from eternity. Though it be granted that it was devised to meet the events that occur, in time, it must have existed from eternity; since those events are as fully comprehended in the divine knowledge from eternity as after their occurance in time. Known unto God are all His works from the beginnings, (or as the distinguished Arminian writer, Mr. Watson, translates it, from eternity).

Let these premises be granted (and we see not how they can be denied) and Predestination comes in like a flood. Now, God's eternal decree, by which He makes all things in time fixed and sure, is nothing but His eternal plan, by which He governs Himself in His relations towards His creatures. And His works of providence and of grace are but the revealment of that eternal plan and, consequently, of His eternal purpose. Is it true that the elements and all inanimate nature are controlled by Him? Then all their conditions and mutations are foreordained by Him before the beginning of time. Is it true that He rules with as sovereign sway in the moral as in the physical world?-That the hearts of all men are in His hands and that He turns them as the rivers of water are turned? - Does He send His Spirit to a certain number and no more and convince them of sin, of righteousness, and of judgment? Call them effectually by His grace-regenerate, sanctify, and save them? And does He do all this in accordance with a plan entertained from eternity? Then it follows that they were predestined to this grace according to the purpose of Him who worketh all things after the counsel of His own will. Has moral evil entered into His system, and do wicked men sin against Him, he not paralyzing their faculties nor changing their hearts? And does He leave some, as vessels of wrath, to hardness of heart and blindness of mind that they might be damned? And does all this occur too in accordance with a plan entertained from eternity? Then it follows that from all eternity He decreed for wise purposes to permit the entrance of moral evil into His system to permit men to use the powers He gave them in opposition to His authority; then, it follows that some were before of old (i.e. from eternity), ordained to condemnation (Jude 4). Finally, it follows that the world, in all its physical and moral details, is just as God designed it to be.

Objection 1. "But does not this make God the author of sin?" Let us get a definite idea of this phrase. What do you mean by the author of sin? Sin is the transgression of the law, and the author of sin is one who is the perpetrator of such transgression. God, in this sense, cannot be the author of sin; nor can the Calvinistic doctrine of Predestination be tortured into such a blasphemous testimony against Him. "But does it not teach that evil entered into His system in accordance with His eternal purpose and that He decreed all the acts of transgression that wicked men are guilty of; does it not, therefore, make Him the approver of sin?" This question is a pertinent one, and we will meet it with all fairness. Predestination does assert that all the wicked acts of wicked men were foreordained before the beginning of time; but yet it as unequivocally asserts that God does not approve of them; since it teaches that He before of old ordained them to condemnation because of those very sins. "But how can God foreordain that of which He does not approve?" I will answer your question by propounding another: How can God, when He possesses infinite power, permit that of which He does not approve? When you have answered my question, you will have furnished an answer to your own. Now that moral evil does exist - that wicked men do sin against God, are facts that are indisputable. This happens either by God's permission or against His consent. Now let my Arminian interrogator take either supposition that he pleases. If he says it happens against God's consent - in spite of God's will, then he robs Him of His omnipotence; if by God's permission, then he too is imperatively called upon to defend his system from the odious consequences which he ascribes to mine. The only difference between us is that he says God permits sin, and we say that He decreed from eternity to permit it. But the question again returns: "How can God decree to permit sin without favoring it?" Let us elucidate this by examples:

1. When the tempter approached our first parents in the garden of Eden, God was not absent and was not an unconcerned spectator of what was transpiring. He might, had He been so disposed, have prevented it by expelling the tempter or by strengthening our progenitors against his temptations. He did neither, however. They yielded to his

wiles, transgressed and fell; and, in consequence, lost the favor of God and were expelled from Paradise. Now does this statement make God the author of sin? Surely not: for He was not the actor of the sin - Does it make Him the favorer of sin? Surely not; for, besides forbidding the act, He exhibited after its occurrence in the most tremendous manner His disapprobation by expelling them from Paradise and pronouncing upon them that awful curse under which their posterity are still suffering. "But if the sin of our first parents was so abhorrent to His mind as it seems to be from His treatment of it, how could He ordain from eternity that it should occur?" Why not shape the question thus: If it was so abhorrent to His mind why did He not prevent it since He had the power? Remove your own difficulty first before you condemn me for not removing mine when it is the same precisely with yours. If it was consistent with the divine character to permit the entrance of evil in time, surely it was not inconsistent to decree from eternity to permit it. Doubtless, it was for reasons known only to the most infinitely wise God that sin was permitted to enter into the world; some of which are manifest even to us. Had sin not entered, God would not have been manifested in the flesh; Christ would not have been preached as the Saviour of sinners; the attributes of God's character would not have been exhibited and harmonized before men by the cross of Christ at which mercy and truth meet together, righteousness and peace kiss each other.

2. Again, take the case of Joseph. His brethren, through envy and hatred, "conspired against him to slay him," but, changing their minds, they sold him to a company of Ishmaelites, who carried him down to Egypt and disposed of him to Potiphar. This act, wicked as it was, was foreordained of God; for we are told (Gen. 50:20) that, though his brethren "thought evil against him, God meant it for good." God ordained the act, just as it occurred, for the accomplishment of ulterior good. Was God therefore the author, i.e. the actor of their sin? Surely not. Did He approve of their conduct? Surely not; for it was in violation of all His precepts that had any reference to the case - He expressly forbid the act perpetrated and punished them for its commission in a marked manner. But yet we are expressly told that "God meant it unto good to bring to pass as it is this day to save much people alive." "But how is it possible for God at the same time to ordain the act and yet disapprove of it?" And yet so it is revealed. We are not reasoning with an infidel now but with an Arminian who,

while he rejects Calvinism, believes in Bibleism. (Perhaps, however, we should except Mr. Reneau who says: "convince me that Christianity tolerates such things, and I will plead its cause no more.") To such, we will propound questions in return: Was not God present when this act was committed? Did He unsuccessfully attempt to hinder it? Did He not freely permit it? Nay, did He not mean that it should occur for good to save much people alive? Is not God, therefore, as much the author of sin on your principles as on the Calvinistic? You admit that God foreknew the act; that He permitted it when He might have prevented it; and, with the Bible, that God meant it for good; and yet that He neither performed nor approved it. How then upon these principles of yours is it possible for God at the same time to permit the act and mean that it should occur and yet disapprove of it? Until you can explain this, do not condemn us for that which we should not escape were we to abandon our ground and come over to yours.

3. Again, take the crucifixion of Christ. No act in the annals of the world was so heaven-daring and wicked as the violence offered to the Lord of glory. But yet God from eternity decreed this event; for grace was given us in Christ Jesus before the world was. For this purpose Christ came into the world, and, ages before the event, the minutest circumstances connected with it were foretold through His prophets. He was delivered to the Jews and Romans by the determinate counsel and foreknowledge of God. It was the will of the Father that the Son should die on the cross. But does that make God the crucifier of Christ? Does that make Him an approver of the murder committed upon that innocent and glorious person? We think that even an Arminian must go as far as we do in reference to that most heinous of all the acts committed by men and believe that the crucifixion of Christ was ordained by the Divine Being from all eternity and that it could not in consequence of God's appointment otherwise than happen. Let him, however, entertain whatever opinion on the subject he may - so that he does not make the Divine Being altogether such an one as we are - it will puzzle him as much as he thinks it does us to explain how it can be true that the crucifixion of Christ occurred not only according to God's foreknowledge but by His determinate counsel, and yet the act did not meet with God's approval. Examples of the same kind, enough to fill a volume, may be selected from the Bible; but let these suffice. (See Ex. 4:21, 7:2-5, 9:12, 10:1,2, 14:7,8; Gen. 45:5,7; Ps. 107:17; Deut. 2:30; Josh. 11:20; Jer. 52:3; II Kings 24:20; Jer. 25:9, 43:10,11, 51:20; Is. 14:4-6, II Sam. 16:10,11; Acts 22:21-22, 4:27,28, 3:17,18, &c.)

It will be seen by what has been said that the Arminian system is just as liable as the Calvinistic to the odious objection that God is made the author of sin. But, worse than this, it lies open to a more valid objection still: that, if He is the author of sin, He has made Himself so without having any definite object in view or, in other words, without any reason for it! Arminians believe (and Mr. Reneau among them) that God not only knew from eternity all things that should occur in time but all things possible and, consequently, He knew that if He created Adam and Eve and placed them in Paradise and permitted the tempter to gain admittance to them in the way he did that they would fall. All this, however, He did knowing that sin would inevitably be committed, and thus evil inevitably enter into the system; and yet that most important event that has ever occurred in time did not occur under His direction nor by His appointment! Again, He knew that if He caused such a being as Judas to live in the time of Christ and preserved him by His providence that he would be admitted into the family of the Saviour and, such things happening as did happen, he would be guilty of the awful crime of betraying his master to the Jews; yet all these things He ordered and permitted without ordaining that Christ should be betrayed and crucified - nay; without even decreeing from eternity to permit it! Thus laying the Divine Being open, as much as Calvinists do, to the charge of being the author of sin and yet denying to him all the attributes of sovereignty and all the characteristics of a reasonable being! Is there not room here for some of that virtuous indignation vented by our author against the Calvinistic system?

Thus it is seen that the consequence of making God the author of sin does not flow from the Calvinistic system because of its difference from the Arminian; and thus it will be seen from the scriptures as well as from Calvinism that God ordains the sinful act and yet disapproves of and punishes it. If our object were merely to defend ourselves against the objections of an Arminian, we might rest the subject here and content ourselves with having closed his mouth; but, as we have a higher object, we will go further and attempt to show to the enquirer after truth that predestination is not only sustained by the Bible but is consistent with sound reason.

It is asserted that God, from all eternity, ordained every sin that is commited but yet is neither the author nor approver of it. How can these things be reconciled? The following remarks, it is thought, will aid us to arrive at a solution of the question.

1. A distinction is to be made, as existing in the divine mind, between the sinful act and the result to be attained by it. The one may be abhorrent to God and forbidden by Him and is sinful, because it is a violation of His law; the other may be good and infinitely worthy of accomplishment. Thus, eating the forbidden fruit was a sinful act, because forbidden by God and, as such, was infinitely abhorrent to Him; while the result attained by it was, in part, at least (and who will venture to say it was not as a whole, taking all things into consideration) a good infinitely valuable. It gave occasion for the advent of Christ; for the manifestation of the divine excellencies; and for the bestowal of that glorious grace which will constitute the theme for the praises of the redeemed, throughout eternity. Again, the outrage upon Joseph was, in the perpetrators of it, an unnatural sin and, as such, offensive in the sight of God; but the result attained by it was good and extorted the gratitude of all those affected by it. Joseph's brethren "meant" it for evil, but God "meant" it for good, to save much people alive. Finally, the crucifixion of Christ was not only a violation of the commands of God against the shedding of innocent blood, but was infinitely heinous as a manifestation of the Jews' hostility to Christ's holiness and was, therefore, an awful act of wickedness; but what Christian is unconscious of the glorious consequences of the crucifixion of Christ? What humble soul does not adopt the language of the Apostle, and say - "God forbid that I should glory, save in the Cross of Christ, by which the world is crucified unto me, and I unto the world."

2. It follows from the above that if God knows that any thing will result in infinite good (as the wicked crucifixion of Christ, for instance), it is not unworthy in Him to decree that it should occur; on the contrary, it is infinitely worthy in Him to do so. Calvinists, therefore, divide the will of God into secret and revealed - the revealed to govern His creatures, the secret to govern Himself; and the latter will be attained, whether men regard or disregard the former. But here two other objections are started: 1st. "Does not this imply an inconsistency in God; as His secret will is sometimes one thing, and His revealed another?" and 2nd. "Is this not saying that God does evil, that good may come?"

1st. To the first, we answer that God's revealed will is always consistent with itself, and His secret will is always consistent with itself. The former is given in His precepts; and all the commands, warning, threatenings, persuasions, &c. are consistent therewith. He never commands anything without sincerely requiring it; and, having commanded it, He never authorizes anything that conflicts with it. His revealed and His secret will have reference to objects that are entirely distinct, and cannot, therefore, be compared together. Thus, as we have shown, His revealed will may be entirely opposed to the violence offered to the Saviour and to the motives and feelings that influenced the Jews in that transaction; and yet His secret will, having another object in view, decreed that event in order that the glorious blessings and results that flow from the atonement of Christ might be secured.

2nd. "Is this not saying that God does evil that good may come?"

God is not the doer of evil - the most that can be said, therefore, is that He permits evil that good may come. Substitute, therefore, for the word 'does', the word 'permits', and the question will stand: "Does God permit evil that good may come?" That He does permit evil is indisputable. Only three suppositions, therefore, can be made in the case: Either He permits it without any objection in view and for no reason at all; or He permits it that evil may come; or He permits it that good may come. The first, if we understand them, is the Arminian view; but which is the most honoring to God? Let the reader judge.

Finally, if there is any difficulty in this subject, it grows out of the connection that exists between the omnipotent and sovereign God and finite and responsible men. God's sovereignty and man's free agency are both revealed in the scriptures and, therefore, should be both believed. And if we cannot reconcile them, it is not because they are irreconcilable, but because the subject is above our faculties. We think it has been shown, however, that if the objection considered above can lie against the Calvinistic system, it can be alleged with as much reason against the Bible: and Calvinism is content to stand or fall with the Bible.

Objection 2. "Does not the doctrine which teaches that God foreordained all things even to the sins that wicked men commit, exonerate the sinner from all blame?" This is akin to the objection considered above, viz: that Predestination makes God the author of sin, and the answer to one is applicable to the other. The point of the objection is that, if the creature does what God in His secret counsels ordained should be done and thus becomes an instrument (though unconsciously) for the accomplishment of God's purposes, no blame can be attached to him, and God has no right to find fault. Exactly such an objection and in the same connection is considered and answered by the Apostle Paul in Romans 3:5,6,7,8, "But if our unrighteousness commend the righteousness of God, what shall we say? Is God unrighteous who taketh vengence?" If our wickedness tends to the glory of God and to the accomplishment of His purposes, would it not be unjust in God to punish us? Certainly not, says he, "God forbid; for then how shall God judge the world?" "But," says the objector, "if the truth of God hath more abounded through my life unto his glory, why am I also judged as a sinner?" "And not rather, " answers the Apostle (as we be slanderously reported, &c), "Let us do evil that good may come." Secret things belong to God; and it is a worthy view of Him that He rules with such an omnipotent sway, then even our rebellion and wickedness cannot happen without His permission and cannot thwart His purposes. His revealed will is the rule of our action; and whenever we violate it thoughtlessly or through enmity to it, we are guilty of sin and are blameworthy, whatever may be the consequence of our act as it relates to God. As well might one say who, with malice aforethought, attempted to injure seriously another whom he hated but was thwarted by the skill or power of the latter and thus the act, that was meant for his injury, was made to subserve his interest in a high degree - as well might such an one say, that he was not blameworthy since his act (though unintentionally) wrought good and not evil. And the case supposed would be more pertinent still, and it would not in the slightest degree affect the moral character of the act, if the assailed, unknown to his adversary, became possessed of his intention before hand and determined to permit it, because he foresaw how he could turn it to a good account. Because the wrath of man is foreseen by God and is made to praise Him, that does not make it the less the wrath of man.That God does ordain particular events and all the minute circumstances connected therewith, and yet men act wickedly in bringing them to pass, is asserted by a multitude of scripture passages. Take the following: "Him being delivered by the determinate counsel and foreknowledge of God ye have taken and by wicked hands have crucified and slain" (Acts 2:23). See again, Matt. 17:12; Acts 4:27,28, 27:23,24,34 and that remarkable passage John 19:11. "Jesus answered, thou couldst have no power at all against me, except it were given thee from above: therefore he that delivered me unto thee hath the greater sin." Our objector, however, differing from the Saviour, would say that, under the circumstances, he had no sin at all!

Objection 3. "But does not Predestination, as explained, destroy free-agency, and make men mere machines?" No, on the contrary, it establishes free-agency. Men are free-agents when they act according to their inclinations. Freedom of action is not opposed to necessity but to compulsion. A being may be necessarily holy or necessarily wicked, and yet a free-agent - nay, a free-agent for that very reason. Thus, God is a free-agent though He cannot sin and Satan though he cannot but sin. And so it is with men. Mr. Reneau cannot act otherwise than violently, illiberally, and uncandidly towards his opponents; yet he is a free-agent notwithstanding. Predestination asserts neither that God makes men serve Him against their consent nor that they disobey Him unwillingly. His chosen people He makes willing in the day of His power and so works in them to will and to do His good pleasure, that they find it to be their meat and their drink to do His will; the rest He leaves to themselves, and, in consequence, they sin against Him freely, and, in following their own inclinations, they work out their own destruction greedily. "But you say God does not infuse into the sinner any active principle of disobedience; how then can he fulfil that which God has appointed, and yet not be a mere machine?" And yet so it is; and my Arminian objector is as much responsible for it as I am. Did not Joesph's brethren act freely in their violence to him? Yet God sent him to Egypt? Did not Pharaoh act freely in refusing to let the Israelites go? Yet God hardened his heart that he might not let them go. Was not the curse which Shimei uttered against David the offspring of the bitter feelings of his heart? Yet God told him to curse David. Did not Absalom and his advisers act in an untrammeled manner in adopting the counsel of Hushai rather than that of Ahithophel? Yet "the Lord had appointed to defeat the good counsel of Ahithophel, to the intent that the Lord might bring evil upon Absalom" (II Sam. 17:14). Did not the Jews act freely in crucifying Christ? Yet He was delivered to them by the determinate counsel and foreknowledge of God.

Objection 4. "Does not Predestination make God a respecter of persons?" He is a respecter of persons who favors some because of their rank, position, or circumstances - who accepts the persons of the rich and the exalted, and rejects the poor and the humble, and vice versa. Now, in the sight of God, all men by nature possess the same moral character; and all those extraneous circumstances which give dignity and excellency in this world's estimation, are as nothing, and less than nothing, in His sight. Not many great, not many mighty, are called by Him; on the contrary, God hath chosen the poor of this world and the weak of this world declaring that it is easier for a camel to go through the eye of a needle than for those who trust in riches and station to enter into the kingdom of heaven. Looking upon all as sinners against Him, He chooses some of every condition - rich and poor, bond and free, male and female - not because of their moral or other character but in spite of it. If any system exhibits God as a respecter of persons, it is the Arminian, which represents Him as electing men because of their character - because of faith and good works foreseen in them.

Objection 5. "But in saying that He, by an immutable decree, fixed the eternal destiny of those who were 'before of old ordained to condemnation (Jude 4), do you not represent God as unjust and cruel?" That part of Predestination which relates to the non-elect is divided by Calvinists into preterition and condemnation; i.e., 1st. God passes by some and leaves them in their sins; 2nd. God condemns and punishes them for their sins. Now in which of these resides injustice and cruelty?

1st. Has not the sovereign of heaven the right to with hold His grace from whomsoever He pleases when all are alike undeserving of it? Is it unjust in God to leave men to themselves - especially too when it is their wish that He should do so? Is there any man in a state of nature that desires the knowledge of God's ways? And has He not a right to do as He pleases with His own? Establish it as a truth that God has no right to leave an immortal being to his own inclinations, and you lay Him under obligations to save every child of Adam - nay, to unpeople Hell itself and to restore the Devil and his angels to that estate from whence they fell.

2nd. Is it unjust and cruel in God to condemn and punish sinners for their transgressions? Under what circumstances then can condemnation righteously be pronounced and punishment righteously inflicted? Is the Judge unjust and cruel who pronounces sentence according to law upon the murderer or other capital offender? "But do you not say that God, for all eternity, ordained, before they committed good or evil, that they should come to this condemnation?" Our statement is that God from all eternity determined to pass by those whom He does pass by and to permit them to sin against Him when He knew that this preterition and permission would result in their continuance in sin, and in their final condemnation and perdition. Now is there any thing in this unjust and cruel? Is it unjust to pass them by? You cannot say so; for you know that He does pass them by. God does not give to all men repentance to the acknowledgment of the truth. You are unconscious of it; but it is God's act that you complain of here under the name of His decrees. According to the Calvinistic system, God's decrees are a rule to govern Him and can have no influence upon the creature for good or for evil unless followed by God's act. Another may decree to take your life; but that will do you no harm unless the determination be followed up by the attempt. Will you say, therefore, looking now to what He does, that it is unjust in God to pass by any one, and withhold from Him His converting and His sanctifying grace? You dare not say so. If then, it is not unjust in God to pass by any one in time, surely it is consistent with His justice to decree to do so from eternity. "But does it not seem cruel in God to make men merely to damn them?" Doubtless, when put in this shape and expressed in this strong language, it seems to you a very "horrid" doctrine. We might object to this statement of it as incorrect: waiving this, however, we will meet you in a different way. What would my Arminian opposer say if I should assert that his system too teaches that God makes men merely to damn them? Let us see: You believe in God's foreknowledge (even Mr. Reneau says he does - following Mr. Watson rather than Dr. Clarke). Known unto God then were all his works from eternity. He knew therefore perfectly long before He created them every individual that would live in sin, die in impenitency, and finally perish. Now, reasoning upon your own principles, was it not cruel in God to create them, seeing He was under no necessity to do so? Why did He give them existence? - for their final happiness? He knew as well, from eternity, as they do after they open their eyes in torment, that they would never attain to happiness. What object then did the Creator have in view in giving being to those who He knew would inevitably sin against Him and go to perdition? We should like much to see an intelligent and candid Arminian look at this question without blinking and answer without evasion. Upon your own principles then, may I not ask: Does it not seem cruel in God to make men (if not merely to damn them, at least) that they might be damned? Upon your principles God created the finally impenitent neither for any purposes of His own nor for their lasting welfare - no benefit accrues to Him nor to His system, and they spend on earth a few precarious days and full of troubles and then enter into a state of endless misery! "Cruelty" unmitigated by an incidental or ulterior good either to the creator or to the created! How "horrid" a doctrine, and how strange and unworthy a view of the infinitely wise and merciful God!

It will thus be seen that while Arminians raise such a hue and cry against Calvinism, their own system is liable to precisely the same objections with others that are greater superaded! It would lead us too far from the course marked out in this professed answer to Arminianism and cause us to trespass unreasonably upon the reader's patience (already we fear, too much tried), to attempt an answer to this objection as coming from other than an Arminian. We refer the reader, however, to an able treatise on this subject by President Edwards, entitled, "God's ultimate end in the creation."

Objection 6. "Does not Predestination render unnecessary the use of means?" No; for it teaches that God ordains the means as well as the end. Thus, He ordains that His people shall enter into eternal life; and, that they might be prepared for this, that they shall be holy and without blame before Him in love, and that this state might be attained, that they shall have faith, which works by love and purifies the heart and overcomes the world; and that they might have faith, that they shall hear the gospel, and, therefore, that it shall be preached. Thus Paul stated to the ship's company that it had been revealed to him that every soul on board should be saved, but yet, when the sailors essayed to lower the boat, Paul said to the centurion and the soldier, except these abide in the ship, ye cannot be saved (Acts 27:21-31). Did the centurion and the soldiers demur at this as inconsistent with the unqualified statement of the angel? No: believing that God had ordained the means as well as the end they cut the rope and thus detained the sailors on board.

Other minor objections are alleged against Predestination; but they can all be resolved into those mentioned above and answered upon the same principles.

Having stated the doctrine and answered the objections to it, let us see what are some of its practical influences.

1st. It tends to produce humility. When we feel that we shape our own destiny - that our own power or wisdom has procured for us our advantages or successes, we are attempted to entertain exalted conceptions of our own importance; but when we believe that God rules above and rules below and works all things after the counsels of His own will - that He not only called us into being, but selected according to His sovereign pleasure, the time and place and circumstances of our existance - circumstances too, that exert a controlling influence upon our destiny - that He chooses out our changes for us and directs our steps - that He acccomplishes His own purposes in our lives, working in us, and by us, for the manifestation of His own glory; we feel that, in the presence of God, we are nothing and less than nothing and vanity.

2nd. It tends to make those engaged in the service of God labor with more diligence. While nothing is more paralyzing that the apprehension that, with all our exertions, we shall fail of the attainment of our object: so, nothing is more stimulating than the assurance that success will crown our well-directed efforts. Now, if predestination be true, we know that God has purposes concerning us and that all those purposes will be infallibly secured. And whenever in a right spirit and in a proper way, we attempt any thing that is in accordance with His revealed will, we are assured that our labor will not be in vain in the Lord. Are we laboring for God's glory by seeking to obey Him in heart and in life? We know that He wills the sanctification of His people, and therefore, we run not as uncertainly, we fight not as those that beat the air. Are we laboring as God's ministers for the salvation of sinners and for the edification of His people? We have the strongest assurance in God's purpose, and God's promises that our sincere exertions will not be unavailing. Though all our unaided efforts will be ineffectual to destroy the enmity in the heart of a single sinner, yet, we know that the Lord has a purpose to accomplish in the preaching of the Gospel and that He has declared His word shall not return unto Him void, but shall accomplish the thing whereunto He sent it. Having, therefore, the conviction that He has called us into the ministry, though set down in the midst of the valley that is full of bones - many and very dry - we can, by the Divine command, prophecy unhesitatingly, and look with confidence, to see "bone come to his bone" and perhaps an exceeding great army standing up on their feet, having in their nostrils the breath of spiritual life (Ez. 37:10)

3rd. It tends to strengthen and support the Christian under all his calamities and sufferings. To the believer of the doctrine, nothing happens by chance, but all things, good or bad, prosperous or adverse, occur by God's direct command or by His express permission. He feels persuaded that His providence ruleth over all and that His hand is to be seen in every thing that happens to him. Does he enjoy prosperity? He thanks God for His goodness. Does he suffer under affliction or calamity? His language is, "It is the Lord, let Him do what seemeth Him good." Job saw the hand of God, not only in those calamities that came directly from Him through the agency of the powers of nature, but in those also that befell him through the agency of violent men; and he submitted to both, as being in accorance with the Divine will (Job 1:8,21). Messengers came to him in haste and informed him that the Sabrans had taken away his oxen and his asses and slain his servants - that fire from heaven had consumed his sheep and his servants - that the Chaldeans had carried away the camels and slain the servants and that a great wind had overturned the house in which his sons and daughters were collected and slain them all. And Job rent his mantel and said, "naked came I out of my mother's womb, and naked shall I return thither, the Lord gave (oxen and asses and sheep and camels and servants and children) and the Lord hath taken away (through the agency in part of predatory and wicked bands of Sabrans and Chaldeans), blessed be the Name of the Lord." The same resignation to the Divine will was exhibited by the company of primitive Christians when they tried unsuccessfully to dissuade Paul from placing himself in the power of the wicked Jews at Jerusalem, who, he was forewarned, would lay violent hands upon him. When Paul had been informed by the prophet, Agabus, that the Jews would bind him hand and foot and deliver him to the Gentiles, the brethren tried to persuade him not to go to Jerusalem, but seeing that their importunity only served to distress him, they ceased saying, "the will of the Lord be done" (Acts 21:14).

To these we may add that it tends to excite gratitude to God in the heart of the believer, who can say, by the grace of God I am what I am and gives to him a solid foundation for Christian assurance when, having the scriptural reason for the hope that is within him, he can adopt exultingly the language of the Apostle, "I am persuaded that neither death, nor life, nor angels, nor principalities, nor powers, nor things present, nor things to come, nor height, nor depth, nor any other creature, shall be able to separate me from the love of God, which is in Christ Jesus my Lord (Rom. 8:38,39).

SECTION III.

We come now to a consideration of the arguments contained in our author's first sermon. We design not to attempt a correction of all the misapprehensions and misrepresentations, with which this "sermon" abounds - to do so would take up too much space and would hardly be worth the trouble. Whatever of argument, however, we find in it, we shall state fairly and in as strong terms as possible and answer it without evasion. After two paragraphs by way of introduction in his characteristic style, our author commences the discussion with "We proceed to consider:"

"First. The difference between Calvinian (?) and Arminian predestination" - This is the "First". We have searched diligently through the production, but have not as yet been able to discover the Second. But let that pass. He then quotes from the Presbyterian confession of faith, a definition of predestination, as he says, but really of election: and, from the works of Arminius, the Arminian definition of the same; strangely confounding words and ideas. Much the largest part of the production, however, is taken up with criticisms, and "arguments" on the subject of foreknowledge. Reserving for the present a review of his remarks on the doctrine of Election, we address ourselves first to his refutation and correction in reference to God's foreknowledge.

"The subject of foreknowledge," he says, "has been a very perplexing one." Yes; we perceive it has been - to him. And if that absurd and ridiculous notion of foreknowledge which he ascribes to Calvinists, gave him so much perplexity, what would have been his condition if he had, by any means, encountered that which Calvinism does teach?

Calvinists maintain, says he, that it is impossible for God to know any thing excepting what He had decreed! (p.3) To prove this, he quotes from Dr. Hopkins and Calvin. The former we shall not defend against his strictures. Whether the sentiments quoted from him conform to our system or not is not material; it is enough to know that he is not recognized as a Calvinist and that we are not responsible for him. The extract from Calvin, however, our author says, expresses the same sentiments and is as follows: "God therefore foreknows all things that will come to pass, because He has decreed that they shall come to pass." Throughout his remarks he confounds in the same way knowledge and foreknowledge. Now, we venture the assertion, that there never was a Calvinist so ignorant and so absurd, as to deny the infinity of God's knowledge. Even Dr. Hopkins, as heterodox as he is on some other points, maintains unequivocally that from eternity God knew all things possible. And we challenge our author or any one else to produce a single Calvinistic writer that denies God's omniscience. As long ago as the time of Augustine, if not before, as the books on systematic divinity will show, the knowledge of God has been divided by those who believe in His decrees, technically, into scientia simplicis intelligentiae knowledge of simple intelligence or of all possible things; and scientia visionis knowledge of vision or of all those things which shall come to pass. "The first is founded upon the omnipotence of God; He knew all things which His power could perform. The second is founded upon His will or decree, by which things pass from a state of possibility to a state of futurition." God knew of innumerable worlds which His power might bring into existence; but He foreknew that this world would certainly exist, because He had determined to create it. God knew that the history of this world might have been infinitely varied; but He foreknew that it would be just as it is, because He decreed that His creating, His upholding, and His governing power should be exercised just as they have been and are. Now what is there is this that denies the infinite knowledge of God? And we defy our author to show that this is not a correct statement of the Calvinistic sentiment.

In reference to God's knowledge, there is no difference of opinion between Calvinists and Arminians - both believe it to be infinite. Nor do they differ as to the extent of His foreknowledge; both believe that He knew from eternity all that would take place in futurity. The precise difference between them consists in this: Calvinists maintain (and it is a fundamental principle upon which the system of Calvinism in all its parts rests) that "the will of the Supreme Being is the cause of every thing that now exists, or that is to exist at any future time;" and they hold, therefore, that God foreknew that certain things would happen in the future, because He had willed that they should. They define God's knowledge to be a clear and intuitive perception of all those things that may be; and His foreknowledge a clear and infallible perscience of all those things which He hath willed to be. The Arminians, on the contrary, deny that the will of God is the cause of those things that exist (at least in the moral world), and maintain that His foreknowledge is a perscience of events, some of which did not enter into His decree and which He had no agency in producing. The former make future things dependent upon God's will; the latter make God's will (as we shall see hereafter) dependent upon future things. The former maintains that God foreknew the future things because He had decreed that they should exist; the latter, that He has decreed nothing about (at least some of) them, and consequently (we may add), they happen independently of His will.

Now, God's decree is synonimous with God's will. Substitute, therefore, in the extract taken from Calvin, the word 'willed' for the word 'decreed', and the Calvinistic idea of foreknowledge will stand thus: "God therefore foreknows all things that will come to pass, because He has willed that they shall come to pass." Or it may be stated in two propositions, thus: 1st. Nothing can come to pass in time except what God wills shall come to pass; 2nd. God foreknows that certain things will come to pass, because He wills they shall come to pass. It will then be perceived that it was incumbent upon our author to controvert this, not by asserting that Calvinists deny the infinite knowledge of God (an assertion that is contradicted by all the Calvinistic writers), but by showing the incorrectness of the fundamental principle, viz: that all things depend for their existence upon the Divine will. We have searched about in the confused mass of observations on foreknowledge, filling seven pages of his pamphlet, and the following are all that we can find in the shape of arguments bearing upon this point.

1. "If God's foreknowledge is dependent on His decrees, the eternity of His foreknowledge is necessarily destroyed." If His foreknowledge depend upon the decree, it would be absurd to suppose He could have that foreknowledge before the decree existed." p.10 Dr. Hopkins had stated that fore-knowledge must be considered as in the order of nature consequent upon the determination and purpose of God: and our author argues against him as if he had said consequent in the order of time! In consequence of the poverty of language, whenever we speak of the Infinite Mind, we are compelled to use terms drawn from the analogy of our own finite minds, which, by those so disposed, can easily be perverted. Now when it is said that God's foreknowledge is, in the order of nature, consequent upon His will, we mean not that it is consequent in the order of time - for God's knowledge and God's will existed from eternity - but that the one depends for its existence upon the other. God's knowledge (or His omniscience) is a distinct and independent attribute and is

infinite; but God's foreknowledge is limited to the apprehension of objects not infinite in number and is dependent upon His will. The argument then may be stated in a nutshell, thus; God's foreknowledge takes cognizance only of future things; but all future things are dependent upon God's will; therefore, God's foreknowledge also is dependent upon His will: and is consequent upon it in the order of nature.

Again, to make it, if possible, plainer still: suppose He had determined from eternity not to bring a universe into existence - not to create any intelligencies, but to continue Himself the sole-existing being: in that case He could have possessed no foreknowledge; for foreknowledge differs from knowledge in the fact that it perceives events before they occur, but, upon the supposition, no events were to occur, and none, therefore, could be foreknown. Upon the supposition made, while He would have possessed infinite knowledge, He would have been entirely destitute of foreknowledge. Why, then, has He possessed foreknowledge from eternity? Because from eternity He willed or decreed that He would create the universe, and that certain events should occur in that universe which could be the objects of foreknowledge.

Now if it be true that, because God's foreknowledge is consequent in the order of nature upon His will, it could not have existed from eternity, the same is true in reference to those things that are consequent in the order of nature upon His wisdom and benevolence. Take, for instance, the plan of salvation - God's purpose of grace towards the creatures He would make. His wisdom devised the plan, and His love prompted Him to send His Son to execute it; and we are distinctly told that this purpose and grace were given us in Christ Jesus before the world was. Now if it were not for God's wisdom and benevolence, the plan of salvation would never have been devised! What then, is the conclusion? - that God did not entertain this purpose from eternity? So our author would say, if he is consistent.

2. Again, to prove that God's foreknowledge does not depend upon His decree, he draws an argument from the analogy of human knowledge. We, says he, foreknew some things as, for instance, we know we must die; and if we should see a man shingling a house by reversing the order - by commencing at the top of the roof, we would foreknow that when it rains that house will leak; and this too without having decreed any thing on the subject! p.4. This is an involuntary acknowledgment that God, in his opinion, is altogether such

an one as we are. To make the analogy complete, however, instead of degrading the Supreme Being to the level of the spectator, he must elevate the latter to the position occupied by the Creator. Let it be supposed then that this spectator was a self existent being, possessing all the attributes of God and stationed at a period anterior to the creation of the universe; for him to foreknow that that house would leak, it would be necessary for him to determine to create the world and to uphold it to the time of the existence of the builder; to give him being at the proper time and place and to preserve his life; to furnish the materials out of which to construct his house; and to cause the vapors to ascend and form the clouds that should discharge themselves upon that foolishly constructed house. Let this be supposed, and a child can see that the foreknowledge of that Being - call him man or God - would be dependent upon his determination or will.

After what has been said above, no answer is necessary to the puerilities, that this Calvinisitic view of foreknowledge makes it synonimous with memory! p.5, and that is equivalent to asserting that God made His decrees in ignorance! p.8. Besides these, his production contains no other arguments against Calvinistic foreknowledge. In conclusion, we will venture the remark that, if he had studied the subject before attempting to write on it, neither himself nor his readers would have been so much perplexed.

The doctrine of election, under the comprehensive name of predestination, receives our author's first and last assault. "Calvinists hold," says he, "that God predestinates His elect without any foresight of faith or good works, or perserverance in either of them or any other thing in the creature, as conditions or causes moving Him thereunto" (See Pres. Confession of Faith, Chap.3, Art. 5. p.1.). The whole article of which this is an extract expresses more clearly the Calvinistic view of the subject: "Those of mankind that are predestinated unto life, God before the foundation of the world was laid, according to His eternal and immutable purpose, and the secret counsel and good pleasure of His will, hath chosen in Christ unto everlasting glory, out of His mere free grace and love without any foresight of faith and good works, or perserverance in either of them, or any other thing in the creature as conditions or causes moving Him thereunto; and all to the praise of His glorious grace." Now our author affects to understand Calvinists by this to say, that personal holiness is not necessary as a qualification for admission to heaven - that God receives men into the kingdom of glory, without reference to their character, i.e. though they may be unbelievers and evil doers! "It is palpable that Calvinists hold, that God's elect are ordained to the everlasting life without any regard to their Christian character, seeing that such character is composed of faith and good works" - p. 14. "Elected without any reference to Christian character, a change of character would not produce the least change in their relation to God." p.15. (We quote from the second sermon, because the idea is more concisely stated; the reader will see the same however more diffusely expressed on pp. 2, 10). And he goes on to argue against this: 1st. That "God predestinates to conformity to the image of His son." p. 10; and 2nd. That " on the last day, men will be judged according to their works." p.11. He argues at length on these points, doubtless, in his opinion, very conclusively; but the truth is they have no relevancy to the case in hand. His opponents hold them to be true no less firmly than he does. The true question at issue he seems not to have conceived at all. In a recent publication he says, he "holds it criminal to misrepresent an author;" the only conclusion left us therefore is that he did not understand that upon which he was writing. And yet the uninitiated would suppose, from the confident manner in which he expresses himself, that he had the subject at his finger's end. Ignorance, while it should always be modest and difident, is not unfrequently self-conceited and presumptuous.

Arminians and Calvinists both believe that men will be judged according to their deeds, and that Christians are purified as a peculiar people, zealous of good works. Both believe that without holiness, no man shall see the Lord; and both believe in a doctrine of election. The precise difference between them is this: Arminians hold that God elects some because He foresees that they will believe in Christ and obey His will: Calvinists, that God, seeing all men, while in a state of nature, possessing the same moral character, and without exception, unbelievers and rebels, without reference to (i.e. in spite of) that character, chooses some to holiness and eternal life, influenced solely by His sovereign benevolence. The former believe that He chooses them because they have faith and good works; the latter that He chooses them that they might have faith, and might perform good works. The former make the sinner take the initiative in his election, and consequently, (we may say) in his salvation, and then introduce the Supreme Being as his coadjutor; the latter make of God the author and the finisher of the sinner's faith, and the originator of every thing good in the creature. In a word, Arminians maintain that faith and good works are the causes of God's election; and Calvinists that they are the effects of it. In reference to the gift of the Holy Spirit, Arminians believe that it is bestowed irrespective of election and upon all in a measure sufficient to secure their repentance and faith - that it can be improved or misimproved, received or rejected, according to the will of the creature, and that God chooses those who, He sees will properly improve its influences; Calvinists believe that it is bestowed subsequently to election, and with the design to make its decree effectual, and, in its influence upon the elect, is invincible.

The true question at issue therefore is, whether election is the cause or the effect of faith and good works. Calvinists believe the former, and maintain that it is sovereign, and is the cause of every thing morally good in the creature. This then is what our author should have attacked, if he had wished to refute Calvinistic election. Everything he has said, that has any bearing upon the point at issue, is sufficiently answered by the simple statement above of the Calvinistic doctrine; but lest he may say that we pass them over because we cannot answer them, we will give them (begging our readers' pardon for doing that which is so unnecessary) accompanied by a formal reply:

1. He asks, "If God knew, at the time He passed the decree, all about their personal character and holiness of heart, why did He not have reference to it? Was there so little difference between vice and virtue in God's account, that his government regarded it not?" p.2. No; but God saw in the character of men in a state of nature all "vice" and no "virtue". His Bible teaches the total depravity of all men. It asserts that they that are in the flesh cannot please God - that the carnal heart is enmity to God, not subject to His law, and unable to be; and, consequently, that none but those influenced by His grace will ever repent, believe and obey. He could not, therefore, elect them because of faith and good works foreseen; for He foresaw that none would believe and serve Him if left to themselves. If elected at all, therefore, they are elected not in consquence of, but in spite of their character: not because they are obedient, but that they might be obedient. And this is the apostle Peter's opinion. "Elect according to the foreknowledge of God the Father, through sanctification of the Spirit unto obedience" (1 Pet. 1:2).

2. Another argument which seems to be leveled at predestination as a whole ,we put in this place for the want of a better, as we wish to reply to all of his arguments, whether he

has properly arranged them or not. He says: "The man who believes the Calvinian notion of predestination, never feels the force or truth of such passages of holy scripture, as teach the universality of the atonement. Tell him that Christ tasted death for every man, he feels in difficulty about the reprobate."p.11. To this, we answer that this embarrassment is altogether imaginary. Calvinists rejoice in the privilege conferred upon them to preach the gospel to every creature. Whether they believe in a general or a limited atonement - whether they believe that Christ died for all men without exception, or only for His elect,(and we are sorry to say that there is a difference of sentiment on this point), they feel no hesitation in calling upon all men, and commanding them in the name of God to repent and believe the gospel, and in pointing all penitent sinners to a crucified Saviour. If they believe that the Bible places a limit to the intention of the atonement, they believe also that it represents its merits to be infinite, and sufficient to save a thousand times the number of the descendants of Adam, if applied to them. They feel no hesitation, therefore - nay, they rejoice to declare to every sin burdened soul: Christ is able to save to the uttermost all that come unto God by Him.

Having thus answered all of our author's arguments that have any bearing upon the doctrine of election, let us see if the war cannot be carried successfully into Africa.

1. The position that the Holy Spirit is bestowed upon all in a measure sufficient to secure their repentance and faith, does not seem to be sustained by fact. The large majority of man-kind live in heathen lands, where not one ray of spiritual light reaches their minds. They have no knowledge of the true God, and of the law which He has published in His word for the government of His creatures, and,consequently, know not when they have sinned against Him by its infraction. True, they have the light of nature, and that law written upon their hearts by the dictates of which their consciences either accuse or else excuse them; but the former is so darkened by superstition, and the latter so confounded with heathenish maxims, as to be insufficient to guide them in the path of duty, or to point them to the path of saftey. Now, in what way can the Spirit, if sent to the benighted heathen, operate upon their hearts? Of what can it convince them? - of sin? But by the law is the knowledge of sin; and they have no law excepting that written upon their hearts, which has been obliterated and displaced by the law of custom and superstition. If they should by any means be convinced by the Spirit that they are sinners, how can they obtain forgiveness of sin? By belief in Christ? But

how can they believe in Him of whom they have not heard? By any other way? But Christ is the only way - there is none other name under heaven given among men whereby they can be saved. It is evident, then, that if any of the adult heathen who have never heard the Gospel are saved, they are saved without faith in Christ, and by a wonderful exercise of the power of the Spirit of God in their behalf. If saved without faith in Christ, then we have some who were elected without a foresight of faith at least, whatever may be true in regard to good works; and if God by His sovereign power can save some heathen without a foresight of faith, why can He not (reasoning upon Arminian principles) save all? And if none of the adult heathen are redeemed while some in gospel lands obtain salvation, what becomes of the doctrine that God treats all men alike? If, in answer to this, it be said, He treats all men alike in the very fact that He gives all His Holy Spirit; we reply that in giving His Spirit to the heathen when He knows that their condition cannot be bettered, but their responsibilities must be increased, and their guilt enhanced by it without the Gospel, He curses rather than blesses them.

2. If men are elected because of their faith and good works foreseen, and thus are made to differ from others, they have room for boasting, and have a right to ascribe their salvation, at least in its incipient stages, to their own merits. If the Holy Spirit be bestowed upon all in a measure sufficient for their salvation, and some improve His influences, while others do not, it is because of some excellencies of character inherent in the former and not in the latter and, consequently, in answer to the Apostle's question, who made thee to differ? they can say, "we made ourselves to differ." And, if any are in this condition, they at least cannot join in the ascription of the redeemed: Not unto us, but unto thy great name be all the praise.

3. If any are chosen because of faith and good works, it follows that they are the authors of election and not God. They have chosen God, and not God them. But the Saviour said to His disciples: Ye have not chosen me, but I have chosen you.

4. The apostle Paul distinctly asserts that men are not chosen because of their faith and good works foreseen or otherwise (Rom. 9:11) "For the children being not yet born, neither having done good or evil, that the purpose of God according to election might stand, not of works, but of Him that calleth; It was said the elder shall serve the younger." Now faith itself is as much a work as repentance, or love, or any other Christian exercise. Obedience to any command is a good

work, and God not only commands us to repent, but to believe the gospel. What testimony on this point can be more explicit than the following? "For by grace are ye saved through faith; and that not of yourselves; it is the gift of God: not of works, lest any man should boast. For we are his workmanship, created in Christ Jesus unto good works, which God hath before ordained that we should walk in them" (Eph. 2:8-10). "God hath saved us, and called us with an Holy calling, not according to our works, but according to his own purpose and grace, which was given us in Christ Jesus before the world began" (2 Tim. 1:9). Arminians say that God has chosen His people because of faith and good works; but the apostle Paul says that He hath chosen them not according to their works, but according to His purpose and grace - and Calvinists say the same.

5. Another, as it appears to us, unreasonable feature of the Arminian doctrine of election, is, that it may after all prove unavailing, and ineffectual. Our author says, p. 13 "Bible predestination does not absolutely secure everlasting life." Their view may be illustrated by example, thus: God foresees that a certain individual at the age of twenty-five will believe and obey and, therefore, He passes a decree of election in his behalf, and, when the time arrives, actually bestows upon him the blessings of that decree; but when he reaches the age of thirty he apostatizes, becomes a blaspheming atheist, and dies in impenitency. Now, from all eternity, God as well foresaw the awful apostasy as He did the faith and obedience. May we not ask then: Does not this statement exhibit God as insincere? Is it not a mockery, and trifling, to adopt formally into His family those who He knows will five years thereafter backslide and go to Hell? Does it not represent Him too as dependent upon the will of the creature, changing every time that he does - now striving to secure the salvation of the sinner, and then disappointed and giving it up in despair - if this sincere attempt, and hopeless disappontment, can be reconciled with the infallible knowledge from eternity that it would result just as it does. And of what benefit is this election to the chosen one? It does not bring him into a state of holiness, for it is a consequent and not a cause; it does not keep him in a state or holiness, for notwithstanding it, he may fall from grace; it does not secure to him eternal life, for in spite of it he may die in a backslidden state and go to perdition. Is it said that if he die while in a state of grace, he will be sure of heaven? But that is not a supposable case - for God, who has fixed the number of his days, knew from eternity that he would live beyond the period of grace, and die after it should be all exhausted. May

we not say then that this is an election neither honoring to God nor profitable to men?

At this point we close out our review of our author's first sermon. We have, as we think, answered all the arguments contained in it; and if any have escaped our notice, it has not been because we have not diligently searched them.

SECTION IV.

Our author's second sermon is an assault upon the doctrine of the Saints' Perserverance. As a production it is a little more creditable than the first, though it is distinguished, in some degree, by the same characteristic chaos and want of arrangement. The same ignorance of his antagonists' sentiments which is so glaring in the first sermon, is not doubtfully manifested in this. It would give us much pleasure to go into a full discussion of the doctrine assailed; but we waive it for the sake of brevity. An extended discussion however, after what has been said on the subject of predestination, is really not necessary; since if it be true, perseverance, follows as a necessary consequence. We shall confine ourselves strictly then to the arguments of our author.

The confession of faith from which he quoted, states the doctrine thus: "Those whom God hath accepted in his Beloved, effectually called and sanctified by his Spirit, can neither totally nor finally fall away from the state of grace; but shall certainly perservere therein to the end, and be eternally saved.

This perserverance of the saints depends not upon their own free will, but upon the immutability of the decree of election." (Pres. Confession of faith, Chap.17).

This asserts two things: 1. Christians do not totally fall; 2. Christians do not finally fall. The chief part of our author's attack is levelled at the first proposition. Let us take them up separately:

1. Those whom God hath accepted in Christ, effectually called and sanctified by His Spirit, cannot totally fall from grace. Against this our author cites the case of David, who, after having been a child of God, was guilty of murder and adultery, and asks, in substance: Did David continue in a

gracious state? Did he not totally fall? Did not God withdraw from him all gracious influences? "If not then Christianity almost tolerates adultery and murder." p.15. "Then one of God's elect can do as he pleases, and God will punish him for it in this world, Universalism-like." p.14. "Then God has abandoned all government over the elect, has absolved them from all responsibility for their conduct, and His grace is designed merely to remove from them the danger of being judged for their crimes." p.16. Our author supplies from his imagination the gross circumstances connected with this case of David; and enlarges upon it with a seeming relish and a disgusting fulness of detail that do not prove it to be a subject uncongenial to his taste. The consequences above, he advances with an air of triumph, as if he thought they cannot be met: but it all results from confounding with the issue things that are entirely irrelevant. Let us see whether we cannot aid him in making the proper discrimination. The question then as he has presented it, illustrated by example, is: Could David commit murder and adultery and not totally fall from grace? It is important that we have a clear idea of what is the true point at issue:

1. The question is not whether Christians ever commit sin. That Calvinists grant - nay, maintain it against Mr. Reneau and those who think with him. We deny the doctrine of Christian perfection, and insist that both scripture and experience teach that every Christian has an evil heart of unbelief that is prone to wander from the living God. We not only grant, therefore, that David committed sin, but maintain furthermore that there is no man that liveth and sinneth not.

2. Nor is the question whether Christians ever backslide. Mr. Reneau may deny that there is such a thing as Christian backsliding, and, to be consistent, he should do so; but Calvinists (and, we think, the generality of Arminians) grant and maintain that Christians are sometimes permitted to wander for a time far from God.

3. Nor is the question whether the transgressions of those sanctified by the Spirit are less heinous in the sight of God than the transgressions of impenitent sinners. On the contrary, Calvinists hold them to be more aggravated, and , consequently, more deserving of God's disapprobation. The law as a rule of life, is as much binding upon Christians as upon sinners, and the gospel and the grace of God do not relieve His people from the obligation to obey it. God requires them to love Him with all the heart, and their neighbors as themselves;

and to show their love to Him by their obedience to His commandments.

4. The question between us is not whether, while committing sin, all the graces of the Christian continue in active exercise. A Christian cannot experience love, and joy, and hope, and peace, while indulging in a known sin. If his heart condemn him, God is greater than his heart and knoweth all things.

5. Nor, finally is the question whether while indulging in sin, he has evidence that he is in a gracious state or affords that evidence to others. While in this condition he makes his calling and election sure neither to himself nor to those who know him.

What then is the question? This: Did David, while in sin, totally lose the grace that was given him in regeneration? Our author maintains the affirmative and Calvinists the negative? Before taking up his objections, we will present two considerations, which, to our mind, are conclusive that the Calvinistic view is correct.

1. That David did not totally lose the grace given him in regeneration is evident from the fact that his state of sin was of temporary duration and that he was speedily rescued from it by repentance and forgiveness. Many others besides David have been guilty of murder and adultery, who have continued hardened and impenitent after detection and reproof; but David, as soon as reproved in God's name by the prophet, repented - why? Because there was a principle within him that temptation had, for the time, overwhelmed, but which asserted its accustomed influence as soon as the evil tide was checked. The powerful monarch, destitute of grace, when rebuked as he was, would more likely have punished the faithful prophet than trembled before him.

2. That a renewed man does not totally lose the grace bestowed, is evident from the declaration of scripture: (1 John 3:9) "Whosoever is born of God doth not commit sin;(or apostatise) for his seed remaineth in him: and he cannot sin, (i. e. continue in it) because he is born of God." The Apostle is speaking of the habit of sinning. The children of God, says he, are distinguished from the servants of the Devil in the fact that the one like their master continue in sin, and the other like their gracious heavenly Father works righteousness and are habitually holy; and if they, by the force of temptation, are enticed into sin, they do not continue in it, because the seed of grace remaineth in them and they cannot continue habitually in sin, because they are born of God. That this is the true

meaning to be attached to the word sin as the apostle uses it here, is evident from another remark (1 John 1:8) "If we say that we have no sin we decieve ourselves, and the truth is not in us." That the constant habit of sin is what he refers to in the first quotation is evident, otherwise he is made to contradict himself. If the word in both connections means the same thing, then there never was any one who was born of God; for if it be true that all commit sin, and those born of God do not commit sin, then it follows that none are born of God. Again, the evidence contained in David's prayer which he uttered while writing under remorse at the time, is also conclusive: "Take not thy Holy Spirit from me." Not give again, but take not away; implying that His influences were, in some degree, still felt. Finally, Peter's sin was just as aggravated as David's, and his fall was just as signal; but was God's grace totally removed from him? What does the Saviour say? "Satan hath desired to have you that he might sift you as wheat, but I have prayed for thee that thy faith fail not."If there was efficacy in the intercession of Christ, Peter's faith did not fail-all of God's grace was not removed from him. Consequently, when the Saviour turned and looked upon Peter, he went out and wept bitterly. Those same meek and forgiving eyes were turned to many of the hardened wretches that thronged the judgment hall. Why did their mild gaze inspire Peter only with Godly sorrow? Because the seed of God's grace was in him alone.

But says our author:

"If David did not totally fall from Grace, then Christianity almost tolerates adultery and murder." But Calvinists says God was displeased with, and punished him for his crimes. "But how? - by sending him to Hell?" No, "The amount of it is then that God's elect can do as they please, and He will punish them for it in this world, Universalism - like" "God absolves His elect from all responsibility for their conduct, and His grace is designed simply to remove from them the danger of being judged for their crimes; and God has abandoned all government over his elect" But not so fast. Let us reason a little, and see if we cannot answer you out of your own mouth. Let us ask you a few questions about this case of David, your favorite example. Before his connection with Uriah's wife, David was a regenerated man, was he not? You have already, in your pamphlet, answered this in the affirmative. He committed the crimes of murder and adultery; did God not punish him for them? If yes - how? by sending him to hell? If no ; then according to your principles, He punished him for them in this world, Universalism - like. Do you say God forgave him because of his subsequent repentance? We say the same. Do you say God's long-suffering was manifested to him in not cutting him down while in a state of sin? We say the same. What then is the difference between us? We both agree that David had been a child of God, that he committed crimes of a dark dye, that God did not immediately send him to Hell, and that subsequently he repented, was forgiven and restored. The precise question between us is, whether, in the commission of these crimes, he totally fell, i.e. lost entirely the grace of God? This you affirm, and we deny. Now, you perceive, it will not do for you to use an argument, with or without an air of triumph, which will apply with as much force against yourself as against us. We both of us say that David, if punished at all, was punished only in this world, and we both of us disclaim Universalism. "But grace" you say "is favor bestowed without compensation." p.13. How then can God consistently continue this favor to David while his conduct made him so undeserving it? In the same way that he bestowed it upon others and upon David in the first instance whose conduct was undeserving it. David did not merit it, we grant; and if he had, it would not have been grace but debt. It was grace, because it was undeserved. "But," you say, "in the very act of continuing His grace to David while guilty of these crimes, did God not abandon all government over him, and give him full license to sin against him with impunity?" No; unless it can be shown that the grace of God has a hardening influence, and that its tendency is to embolden men in transgression. Now we grant that forebearance towards the sinner does frequently tend to harden. The Bible states that: "Because sentence against an evil work is not executed speedily the hearts of the sons of men are fully set in them to do evil." If therefore, you substitute in your question the word forebearance for the word grace it would have some pertinence. But that question you cannot propound to us; since you, no less than we acknowledge that God exhibited forebearance towards David. The tendency of God's grace is not to harden but to soften the heart, not to encourage in sin but to bring to repentance, and consequently, we find it producing that effect speedily in the case of David. "But was not David's offence most flagrant? How then could God omit to inflict eternal punishment upon him (or at least subject him to the danger of it) without, at the same time, abandoning all government over the elect?" Upon the same principles, my dear sir, upon which he was able, without this consequence, to forgive you and me, (as I trust He has, when our sins had been so flagrant and aggravated against Him, previous to our repentance.) We have found the atonement of the Lord Jesus Christ sufficient for us, and the same great atonement was sufficient for David. God's plan is such that He is just while he justifies the ungodly. His justice is not impugned because He forgave us, nor is it to be impugned in the case of David. We find when we sin that we have an advocate with the Father Jesus Christ, the righteous, and David believed and acted upon the same blessed assurance. The objection rests upon the supposition that the honor of God requires that He should condemn to Hell the sinner, immediately upon the commission at least of (what we would call) great crimes; but is it necessary for us to remind the minister of the Gospel whose views we are controverting, that, in consequence of the sacrifice of the cross, God deals with us not according to our sins, nor rewards us according to our transgressions - that one of the glorious features of the Gospel of Christ, is, that it represents God as "the Lord God, merciful and gracious, long-suffering and slow to anger?" God does not cut men down as soon as they transgress His law, and both we and our antagonist have reason, from our hearts, to thank Him that He has devised a more gracious way to maintain the honor of His law. His own honor and the authority of His law are maintained while He gives transgressors time and space for repentance.

Our author compares Calvinists to Universalists, because they say that the elect are punished only in this world; but the Holy Spirit asserts the same: (Ps. 89:29,30-33), "His (the spiritual David's) seed also will I make to endure forever, and his throne as the days of heaven. If his children forsake my law, and walk not in my judgments. Then will I visit their transgression with the rod and their iniquity with stripes. Nevertheless, my loving kindness will I not utterly take from him nor suffer my faithfulness to fail."

Our author's view of the Christian's sin is peculiar, differing even from the generality of Arminian's "The idea" he says, "that a man can be a child of God and commit sin, is preposterous" p.23. Consequently, whenever a Christian commits sin he falls from grace, and God, for the time being, abandons him entirely. Now as all men, through the weakness of the flesh, and through manifold temptations are constantly liable to sin, and as all Christians perhaps do sin daily, it follows that every Christian totally falls from grace and apostatizes many times every day! And it follows that there is no such thing as backsliding among Christians; they are either elevated to the condition of perfect sanctification or fallen into the state, as far as they know, of hopeless apostasy.

Our author may not be aware of it, but this opinion of his places him in the ranks of Hopkinsians - the very people that he came so near killing by mistake!

Those whom God hath accepted in Christ, effectually called and sanctified by His Spirit, cannot finally fall from grace. Calvinists argue this from the perfections of God; from the immutability of His decrees; from the covenant of redemption between the Divine Persons of the Trinity; from the covenant of grace which God has made with His people; from the atonement of Christ by which He paid the full price for the redemption of His people; from Christ's intercession; from the inhabitation of the Spirit; and from the distinct and explicit declarations of the scriptures. Only two of these our author refers to, viz: 1. The covenant of grace; and 2. The atonement of Christ, but in such terms as not to render it necessary for us (confining ourselves strictly, as we profess to do, to his arguments) to notice them at length.

1. He would seem to maintain that God never made any covenants with man - that there was no covenant of works before the fall, and no covenant of grace since. He says, "Calvinists teach that the elect have been placed under a covenant of grace where they received a benefit which relieves them from obedience to any law (!) But the poor reprobate is left under the covenant of works, the requirements of which, since the fall, are of such a character that neither they, nor the elect are able to comply." p. 16. He gives this not as an inference which he draws from our teaching, but as the very teaching itself! We have already said, in a previous number, that Calvinist maintain that it is the duty of all, elect or non-elect, to observe the moral law as rule of life, i.e. to love God supremely and their neighbors as themselves; and we had thought that every smatterer in Theology knew that all who hold a covenant of works believe that it was abrogated as soon as it was violated, i.e. when Adam sinned. While all since the fall are commanded to observe the moral law as a rule of life, all are told that by the deeds of the law shall no flesh be justified; and that Christ is the end of the law for righteousness to every one that believeth. The commandment to all is not, Do this and live; but, Repent and believe the Gospel. Now the Covenant of Grace which God has made with His people, and which constitutes the present argument, stands thus: "And I will make an everlasting Covenant with them, that I will not turn away from them to do them good; but I will put fear in their hearts that they shall not depart from me" (Jer. 32:40).

2. From the hints our author throws out in reference to the atonement, it would seem that he is not only in part a Hopkinsian, as we showed in the last number, but in part a Socinian also. He seems to deny that Christ's sufferings were vicarious. "Calvinists hold, " says he, "that the sins of the elect are not transferred to Christ, but they are so imputed to him that he suffered the penalty without being guilty of the crimes committed by his people; and they hold that Christ's righteousness is not really transferred to the elect, but that it so imputed to them that they will stand justified in the day of judgment, their crimes to the contrary notwithstanding(!). We must say we think this a distinction without a difference." p.17. He says this is a "silly notion of transferred punishment without the transfer of the crimes for which it was inflicted." This would seem to imply that, in his opinion, Christ was not our substitute; that our guilt was not so charged to his account as that he was made answerable for it. Yet the Scriptures state: That "He was made sin for us;" that our "iniquities were laid upon him;" that "he bore our sins in his body upon the tree;" that "we are made the righteousness of God in him," and that "by his stripes we are healed." Our author has left this point so obscure that we know not whether we are required to answer an Arminian or a Socinian argument. Calvinist maintain that Christ is the surety for His people; and having, in the atonement, paid all their debt, He has released them from the obligation to pay it themselves. If Christ made satisfaction for the sins of His people, they are forever exempted from the necessity of suffering the punishment due to their sins. "In consequence of the atonement of Christ, then, will the elect be taken to heaven, their crimes to the contrary notwithstanding?" No, they will be purified from these, and thus prepared for heaven; for Christ is elevated a prince and a Saviour to give repentance to Israel and remission of sins.

To prove that Christians can finally fall, our author, in the next place, quotes a number of passages from the Scriptures. Let us see if these will avail him any more than his other arguments:

And first, the passage which he has selected for his text: "We then as workers together with him, beseech you also that ye receive the grace of God in vain" (2 Cor.6:1). Now even an English reader, by noticing the context, can see that this exhortation is addressed to the ministers in the Corinthian church. Dr. McKnight translates correctly from the original thus, "Now, fellow-laborers, we also beseech you not to receive the grace of God in vain." "The grace of God in this passage signifies, not only the office of the ministry, but the spiritual gifts bestowed upon the ministers at Corinth to fit them for their office." (1 Cor. 3:10). But even if it be granted that the exhortation is more general: the grace of God even then would not mean regeneration, and sanctification but "the gospel offers of reconciliation" (See 5:18-21).

The next three passages quoted are taken from parables and metaphors. Now there is no doctrine, however unscriptural, which cannot be plausibly supported by arguments drawn from the phraseology of parables and metaphors when they are taken out of their connection. A parable should be used merely as the illustration of the particular point with which it is connected. Its dress and embellishments are designed only to make it a complete parable, and for no other purpose. A controversialist is "hard pressed" when he has to sustain his system of theology by a resort to parables taken out of their connection. Does our author say we take this ground because they testify against us? We shall see if he will not be disposed to take the same ground for his protection before we are done.

His first is (Matt. 5:13) "Ye are the salt of the earth." &c. The phrase which, in his opinion, proves falling from grace, is: If the salt have lost his savor, &c. Now, if this clause proves his doctrine, the next proves too much for him; since it asserts, according to his method of interpretation, that those who sin can never be recovered: Wherewith shall it be salted? And to prove that those who have received the grace of regeneration may perish in Hell, he cites: Is it thenceforth good for nothing but to be cast out &c. Out of what? Why not with as much reason, out of the church as out of heaven? The literal meaning of the passage is this: It is designed that the professed followers of Christ should exert a salutary influence upon the world, but if, in doctrine, or in life, they exert a contrary influence, they are to be expelled from the communion of the faithful, and treated as other ungodly men.

His second is (Matt. 12:43, &c) "When the unclean spirit is gone out of a man," &c. Dr. Adam Clarke, (good authority we suppose with Mr. Reneau) acknowledges that the design of parables was "to point out the real state of the Jewish people, and their approaching desolation." But suppose it refers to individuals: It is then designed to describe the case of those who are convinced of the truth, partly reformed, but not truly converted. The unclean spirit had gone out of the man, but his heart had not become the habitation of the Spirit: it was empty. When its former occupant returned, he found it

His third is (John 15:1-11) "I am the true vine, and my father is the husbandman," &c. Over this he exults as much as over any other, and thinks he has made it so plain that "furher comment is needless;" but so little effect have his remarks upon us, by way of conviction, that we would choose this as a passage to prove perserverance. Let us see: "Every branch in me that beareth not fruit he taketh away: and every branch that beareth fruit, he purgeth it, that it may bring forth more fruit." (v 2). Here we are told 1. That there are two kinds of branches in Christ, those that bear no fruit, i.e. those nominally, by profession, united to Him; and those that bear fruit, i.e. those spiritually united to Him; and we are told, 2. What is done to each of these two classes of professors. The former are taken away: the latter are purged that they may bring forth more fruit. Genuine Christians then (fruitful branches) are in the hands of the Father (the Husbandman), and He prunes them or removes from them all those things which hinder their fruitfulness with the design that they may continue increasing in fruitfulness to the end. If this is not perseverance, we know not what is. Our author, however, denies that mere nominal professors are referred to at all; for such, says he, cannot be said to be in Christ. All that are in Him have been united to Him by faith. But the Apostle Paul thought differently. He says that all the members of the church in Thessalonica(I Thes. 1:1) and all the members of the churches in Judea were in Christ (Gal. 1:22), meaning, of course, in a judgment of charity and by profession. But, says our author, Christ says (v.3) to the disciples, Now ye are clean, and subsequently "teaches that they may become unfruitful branches, and be cast into the fire." The truth of this is not as evident to us as it seems to be to Mr. Reneau. In the first quotation, the emphatic word in now. In a previous chapter (13:10,11), He had said to them, "And ye are clean, but not all. For he knew who should betray him; therefore said he, ye are not all clean." After the departure of Judas, the exception was no longer made; and He testified, Now ye are clean. After this testimony He does not, even in hypothesis, suggest the possibility that His disciples could fall away. "What, does he not say, If ye abide not in me ye are cast forth and burned?" No; He says if a man abide not in me, &c. applicable not to the disciples but a general remark applicable to those who are in Him only by profession. We take the liberty, therefore, to suggest to our author that, in order that he may sustain his position by this passage, "further comment is needed."

The passage (I Cor. 10:1-12) "Moreover, brethren, I would not that ye should be ignorant how that all our fathers were under the cloud," &c., we are willing to submit to the reader with the briefest possible comment. Our author assumes that all the Israelites that came out of Egypt were Christians, because they all eat the same spiritual meat and drank the same spiritual drink! Now we beg our readers pardon for explaining a thing so obvious. The meat referred to was manna which was a type of the spiritual bread from heaven (John 6:5,8), and the water was that which gushed forth from the rock, which was a type of Christ. After the interpretation, which makes all the Israelites Christians, he prepares us for any thing, however extravagant; we are not surprised, therefore, when we learn from him that the apostle meant by the word fell, not only that the three and twenty-thousand died, but fell from grace in one day! pp. 20, 24. "Further comment is needless."

His next quotation is, (2 Pet. 2:20, 22) "For if after they have escaped the pollutions," &c. He argues that these were genuine Christians: 1st. "because they knew the way of righteousness." To this we answer that it is applicable to all who know the theory of the Gospel, or as the Apostle Paul expresses it, who have "received (in theory) the knowledge of the truth." 2nd. "They had escaped the pollutions of the world through the knowledge of Christ." This can, with the strictest propriety, be said of nominal professors, who have not been savingly renewed in the spirit and the temper of their minds. Through the influence of the truth, they may, for a time, reform, and thus escape the pollutions of the world, and yet very naturally become again entangled therein; for it happens, to those whose natures are not thoroughly changed, according to the proverb: "The dog is turned to his own vomit again, and the sow that was washed, to her wallowing in the mire." 3rd. "They walked by the holy commandment delivered unto them." Peter does not say so. He says they knew, (i.e. understood) the commandment, but turned from (i.e., refused to walk by) it.

The next quotation (I Chron. 28:9) we refer to the reader without comment.

His last proof text is (Ez. 18:24), "When the righteous turneth away," &c. Now the question is, does the prophet speak of one who is truly righteous - who is clothed with the righteousness which is of God through faith in Christ? The Bible must not be so interpreted as to make it contradict itself. Can a truly righteous man permanently turn away from his righteousness? John answers in the negative (I John 2:19): "They went out from us but they were not of us; for if they had been of us, they would no doubt have continued with us: but they went out, that they might be made manifest that they were not all of us." The person spoken of by the Prophet is one who passes for a righteous man and thinks himself one but is not really so. The general proposition, that when any man continues to the end doing the abominations that the wicked man doeth he shall die, is denied by no one and least of all by Calvinists. But God's people will not do so; for we are told that they are kept by the power of God through faith unto salvation.

Our author's last argument is drawn from examples given in the Scriptures. Adam and David and Judas and Hymeneus and Alexander were Christians and fell; therefore, says he, others also may fall. The first two are acknowledged to have been recovered again and may, therefore, be left out of the account since they did not finally. Before he can cite Judas as a case of final apostasy, it is incumbent upon him to prove that he ever was a genuine Christian; and it is sufficient for our argument to show that he has failed to do this. He says: "1st. Judas was given to Christ. To be given to Christ is a distinguishing characteristic of the elect." "Those that thou gavest me I have kept, and none of them is lost, but the son of perdition; that the Scripture might be fulfilled"(John 17:12). Now the context shows that "Judas is not mentioned here as an exception, but by way of opposition or distraction: as the woman of Sarepta is distinguished from the widows of Israel, and Naaman, the Syrian, from the lepers in Israel" (Luke 4:25-27). In v. 6, the Saviour says, "I have manifested thy name unto the men which thou gavest me out of the world, thine they were, and thou gavest me, and they have kept thy word." Now if in v. 12 Judas is mentioned as an exception, the Saviour contradicts himself; for in v. 6, he testified that those given to him had, without exception, kept God's word. The true rendering of the passage is none of them is lost, but the son of perdition is lost. Our Saviour's prayer affirms that those given him by the Father, he kept; but Judas was not kept - that none of those given to him was lost; but Judas was lost - that those given to him kept God's word; but Judas did not keep God's word; therefore, so far from showing that Judas was given to Christ, in the sense referred to, it implies very strongly the contrary.

2nd. "Judas was regenerated." To prove this, he cites Matt. 19:28, "Verily I say unto you, that ye which have followed me, in the regeneration, when the Son of man shall come in the throne of his glory, ye also shall sit upon twelve thrones judging the twelve tribes of Israel." Now the thing to be proved here, (even reading the passage as our author does), but which is assumed, is that Judas followed Christ in faith and love and obedience. The passage, if it testifies any thing at all on this point, like the others cited above testifies that Judas was not regenerated. All that followed Christ were to sit upon thrones; but Judas was not to sit upon a throne; the inference therefore is very strong, that Judas never did follow Christ in faith and love and obedience. Besides, it is thought that the proper reading of the passage is, verily, I say unto you, that ye which have followed me, in the regeneration, i.e. when the Son of man shall come, &c.

3rd. "Judas was the familiar friend of Christ and the Saviour trusted in Him" (Ps. 41:9). If by this is meant that he was the bosom friend of Christ and that He confided in him, it cannot be true; for we are told (John 6:64), "Jesus knew from the beginning who should betray him." The specific testimony of Christ goes rather to show that Judas never was a Christian and that He never confided in him. "Jesus answered them, Have not I chosen you twelve, and one of you is a devil? He spake of Judas Iscariot, the son of Simon," &c. (John 6:70,71). And the character, which the evangelist John ascribes to him, does not accord with that of a Christian. "This he (Judas) said, not that he cared for the poor; but because he was a thief," &c. (John 12:6). Besides, it is said that he was "the son of perdition" and that he "went to his own place." It must first be proved that Judas ever was a Christian before he can be cited as one who finally fell.

Hymeneus and Alexander, then, are the only examples left to prove final apostasy. What evidence have we that these were truly regenerated men? Our author says they had faith and a good conscience (I Tim. 1:18-20). But Simon the sorcerer "believed", while "his heart" was "not right in the sight of God;" and he was "in the gall of bitterness and in the bond of iniquity;" (Acts 8:13-23), and Paul possessed a good conscience before he was regenerated (23:1). The faith referred to here was not the grace but the doctrine of faith, (see ch. 3:9 and 4:1 and 5:8) and men destitute of the grace of God may have a good conscience as it relates to their general conduct among men. The doctrine of faith made shipwreck of by Hymeneus was the doctrine of the resurrection (II Tim. 2:17,18) and Alexander the coppersmith did the Apostle much evil. But granting that faith and a good conscience are to be taken in the highest sense; the evidence that these ever possessed them is not to be found in the phrase, having put away; since we can not put away that which we have never had. The Jews (Acts 13:46) put from them the word of God, where the sense is, they rejected or refused to receive. And the word is the same (in the original) in both passages.

We have thus performed the task we have undertaken, with what success the reader will judge. If we have succeeded in teaching our author and others like him a profitable lesson and if what we have written shall tend to confirm the wavering or to establish our brethren in the faith once delivered to the Saints, we shall not consider that our time and labor have been spent in vain.

BOOKS HIGHLY RECOMMENDED

THE REFORMED DOCTRINE OF PREDESTINATION,
Loraine Boettner
(Presbyterian & Reformed Publishing Company)

A. W. PINK — PREDESTINATION
Richard P. Belcher
(Richbarry Press)

MANUAL OF THEOLOGY AND CHURCH ORDER
John L. Dagg (first writing Southern Baptist Theologian)
(Gano Books - Sprinkle Publications

ABSTRACT OF SYSTEMATIC THEOLOGY
James P. Boyce (principal founder of the Southern Baptist
(Seminary now at Louisville, Kentucky)
(Christian Gospel Foundation)